Rail Around Birmingham

CENTRAL BIRMINGHAM

▲ A 1905 LNWR postcard depicting the L&BR's 'Birmingham Station' at Curzon Street at its opening. *Author's collection*

RAIL AROUND BIRMINGHAM

CENTRAL BIRMINGHAM

ANDREW DOHERTY

FOREWORD BY PETE WATERMAN

• RAILWAY HERITAGE •
from
The NOSTALGIA Collection

First published in 2007

British Library Cataloguing in Publication Data

A catalogue record for this book is available from the British Library.

ISBN 978 1 85794 298 9

Silver Link Publishing Ltd
The Trundle
Ringstead Road
Great Addington
Kettering
Northants NN14 4BW

Tel/Fax: 01536 330588
email: sales@nostalgiacollection.com
Website: www.nostalgiacollection.com

Printed and bound in the Czech Republic

Acknowledgements

There are many people to thank who have helped me immeasurably with both my research and development of the Rail Around Birmingham website, and in the additional work undertaken for this book, and if I miss anyone out, please forgive me.

I would like to thank Mark Norton for his continual help and encouragement, and for allowing me access to his late father's incredible photograph collection; Paul Walker, of the West Midlands Exploration website, who has also been of continual encouragement and a staunch sounding-board for many of my ideas; Andrew Smith, of the Malvern Industrial Archaeology Circle (MIAC); and Will Adams, Editor at Silver Link Publishing, for having faith in the project.

A big thank-you too to all those who have gone out of their way to provide me with photographs for use in this publication, most notably Roy Dillon, David Bathurst, Roger Carpenter, Roger Shenton, Kidderminster Railway Museum, Charles Steele, Paul Baxter, Frank Jennings, John Edgington, Paul Walker, Michael Musson, Bob Essery and Terry Walsh.

But my final thanks, and the dedication of this book, must go to my wife Vicky and son Christopher who have endured many years of family outings somehow always ending up at the site of a disused railway, and many hours with me ensconced in my office writing text, reading maps and books and scanning photographs for this publication. To them I say: 'See, I told you I wasn't the only person who was interested in old railways!'

Contents

Preface

This book grew out of a website project I began in 2003 with the aim of documenting the Halesowen Railway through Longbridge and Rubery. As I began to research that small stretch of long-gone railway, a stretch of line I used to play on as a child before all trace was removed by the building of the Frankley housing estate, I became increasingly interested, and concerned, at the sheer scale of the loss of railways that had been suffered in the region. As I looked deeper into the subject I found that nearly half of the railway stations of Birmingham, and indeed of the West Midlands, had been lost, many accompanied by the lines upon which they once stood.

The guiding principle for this book is that it is not intended to be a factual encyclopaedia of the region's railways, but a photographic tour of all the station sites within the County Borough of Birmingham, taking the boundary as it was at railway nationalisation in 1948.

I have aimed to provide a book that guides the reader along all the routes radiating from Birmingham, including: some brief historical information on each line; pictures showing the railway as it is today and how it was yesterday; many never-before-published historical photographs; Ordnance Survey map co-ordinates, should any readers wish to visit any of the sites for themselves; and contemporary photographs taken by myself over the past five years.

I hope it is an enjoyable journey, both nostalgic for those who remember and of interest to those who do not, and that it will serve as a document attesting to the disregard with which a means of transport that was respected and exported throughout the world, and played an integral part in the Industrial Revolution and two World Wars, has been treated in the post-war years, the folly of which is only now truly being appreciated.

▼ Halesowen Railway trackside remains in the undergrowth of Balaam's Wood at the site of Rubery station. *15 June 2007*

Foreword by Pete Waterman

I still remember the first visit I made to Birmingham as a young lad in the early 1950s.

The area was still suffering from the aftermath of the war, but despite this I thought it was a fantastic place, and there were railways everywhere! As I stood at New Street I heard someone say that they were off to Saltley shed, so I tagged along. Now, if you were to put me in an engine shed today, believe me, I would go dreamy, so imagine how I felt at that young age! It was a whole new world for me and I was totally absorbed – in fact, I was oblivious to anything or anyone until, to my horror, I found myself all alone! Panic set in and I have to confess to being close to tears because I was only young and I knew that I had to get back to New Street otherwise I'd be in big trouble at home for wandering off! Trains I love, but exploring...? Well, I felt a bit like Dr Livingstone in the Dark Continent! I can't remember how, but I did manage to walk back, and over the years I perfected the art of wandering off and found my way to all the sheds around Birmingham. It became a weekly pastime, with Tyseley being my favourite place to be – and that hasn't changed either. I still love going to Tyseley not least because I get so well looked after, even after all these years.

For those people who've never visited Snow Hill, and therefore can never understand the spell it cast, I can promise you it was a station that made you feel welcome, and for me, reading this book, the magic of it returns and makes me feel that the next time I pass by I will stop – just to see what's over the wall!

This book has re-awakened memories long since forgotten and my only sadness, I think, is that it's a shame to see in the illustrations that some places are even more run-down today than they were shortly after a war!

It's a great read about a great subject in a great city – who could ask for more?

Dr Pete Waterman OBE
Chair of the LNWR

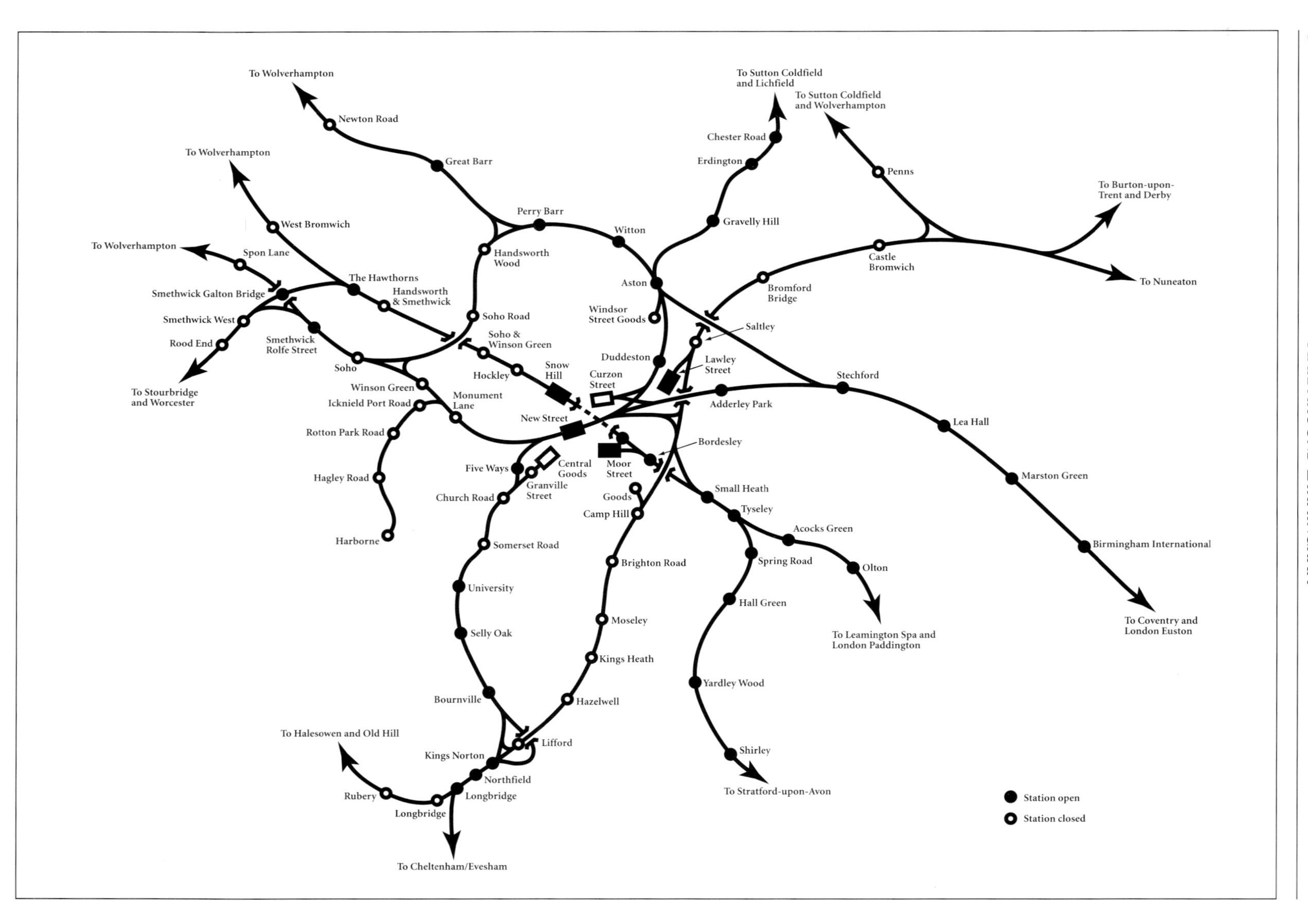

To Wolverhampton
Newton Road
Great Barr
To Wolverhampton
West Bromwich
Perry Barr
Witton
Handsworth Wood
To Wolverhampton
Spon Lane
The Hawthorns
Handsworth & Smethwick
Smethwick Galton Bridge
Smethwick West
Rood End
To Stourbridge and Worcester
Smethwick Rolfe Street
Soho
Soho Road
Soho & Winson Green
Hockley
Snow Hill
Winson Green
Icknield Port Road
Monument Lane
Rotton Park Road
Hagley Road
Harborne
New Street
Five Ways
Central Goods
Granville Street
Church Road
Somerset Road
University
Selly Oak
Bournville
To Halesowen and Old Hill
Kings Norton
Lifford
Northfield
Longbridge
Rubery
Longbridge
To Cheltenham/Evesham
To Sutton Coldfield and Lichfield
To Sutton Coldfield and Wolverhampton
Chester Road
Erdington
Penns
Gravelly Hill
To Burton-upon-Trent and Derby
Castle Bromwich
To Nuneaton
Aston
Bromford Bridge
Windsor Street Goods
Saltley
Duddeston
Lawley Street
Curzon Street
Stechford
Adderley Park
Lea Hall
Bordesley
Moor Street
Goods
Camp Hill
Small Heath
Tyseley
Acocks Green
Marston Green
Birmingham International
Brighton Road
Spring Road
Olton
Hall Green
Moseley
Kings Heath
Hazelwell
Yardley Wood
Shirley
To Stratford-upon-Avon
To Leamington Spa and London Paddington
To Coventry and London Euston
Station open
Station closed

Introduction

From the inception of the Industrial Revolution, Birmingham was well placed to reap the rewards of the developing industries. Not only was the area replete with natural water, surrounded by the Severn and the Trent, together with many more minor watercourses, which provided both a means of transportation and power for the early industrial processes, it also sat on deposits of coal – the fuel for the Revolution proper – and was conveniently sited in Central England and thus a focal point for the emerging national transportation network.

The 'City of a thousand trades' developed rapidly, together with the neighbouring Black Country, into the hub of England's booming industrialisation. Initially, the movement of goods and raw materials was by means of the canal system, which was rapidly developed following James Brindley's completion of the Birmingham Canal in 1773, to the extent that it was said that Birmingham had more miles of canals than Venice! However, the need for a more rapid means of transporting raw materials to Birmingham, and finished products outwards, was to be only truly satisfied by the coming of the railways.

The first railway to arrive in Birmingham was the short-lived Grand Junction Railway (GJR) in 1837, whose line from Warrington passed through Bescot and Perry Barr to a temporary terminus at Vauxhall (now Duddeston). The following year was to see the London & Birmingham Railway (L&BR) arrive in the centre of the town, its line from London Euston terminating at a new station at Curzon Street. In 1839 the GJR extended its line from Vauxhall to Curzon Street, establishing a terminus adjacent to that of the L&BR.

Such was the competition to establish transport links with the industrial capital of England that in 1839 a third company, the Birmingham & Derby Junction Railway (B&DJR), arrived with a line linking Derby and Hampton-in-Arden, a route that necessitated using some of the L&BR's track. However, the B&DJR's arrangement with the L&BR became financially unacceptable and a solution was found in the completion of the Derby company's own route into Birmingham, via Whitacre, terminating at a new station at Lawley Street, opened in 1842.

In 1841 the Birmingham & Gloucester Railway (B&GR) arrived via the Lickey Incline and the Camp Hill line, originally reaching no further than Camp Hill, but later using the L&BR's tracks into Curzon Street to gain the centre proper. The completed B&GR line into Birmingham provided a fast link between the industrial Midlands and the docks at Bristol, a link that had previously taken almost a week to navigate by canal!

Following a flurry of mergers in the 1840s – the Midland Counties Railway, the North Midland Railway and the Birmingham & Derby Junction Railway formed the Midland Railway in 1844, and the L&BR, GJR and the Manchester & Birmingham Railway became the London & North Western Railway (LNWR) in 1846 – together with the expansion of the Great Western Railway (GWR), which had acquired many small railway companies around Birmingham and the Black Country, the Birmingham railway scene was set.

The following years were to see the LNWR and Midland open a new terminus at New Street, and in the process ring the death knell for Curzon Street and Lawley Street as passenger concerns (in 1854 and 1851 respectively), with the GWR developing a strong foothold at Snow Hill.

With the railway now seen as *the* means of transport, lines quickly fanned out across Birmingham and the Black Country – passenger lines, goods lines, colliery lines, lines to industrial premises and private railways, all serving to create a rich, diverse and complex network of rails across the region.

While there were a few early casualties of the fledgling railway era – some over-enthusiasm on behalf of certain railway companies led to passenger lines and stations being built through areas where virtually no one lived or wished to use them – it was not until the 20th century that any

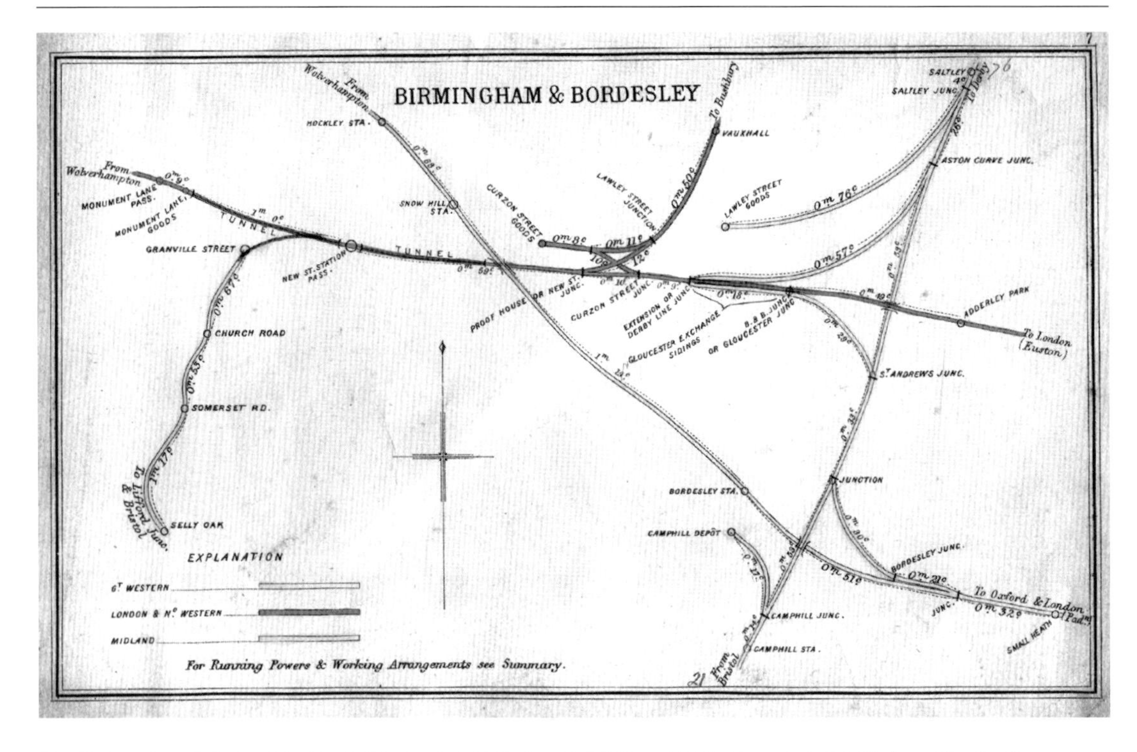

▲ A 1935 Railway Clearing House diagram of Central Birmingham. *Author's collection*

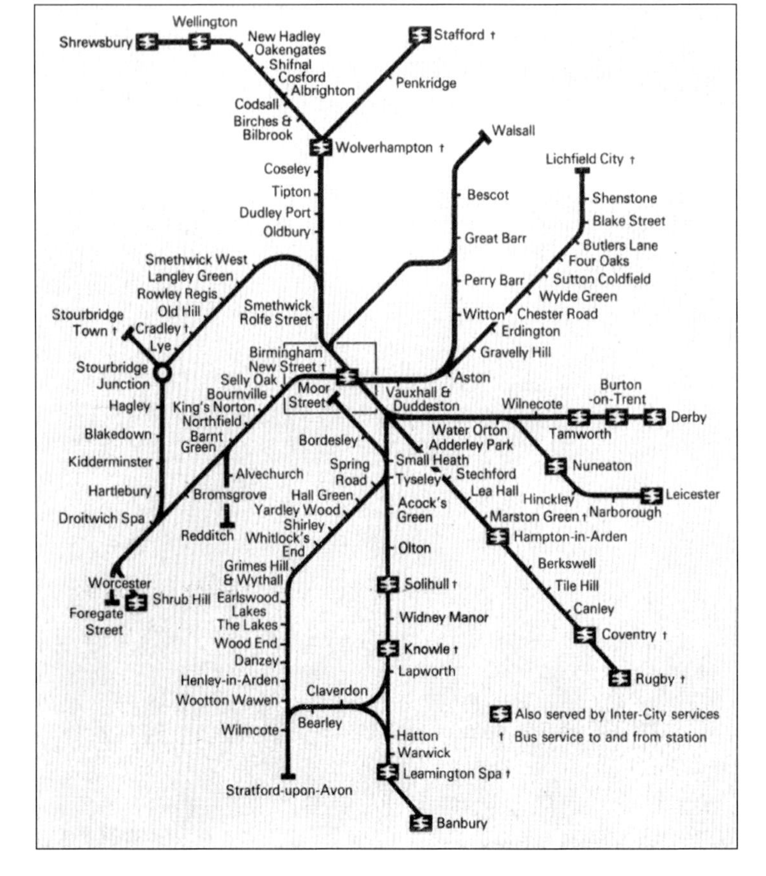

◀ A West Midlands Passenger Transport Executive map from December 1973, showing just how many railway stations and lines had been lost since the turn of the century. *Author's collection*

great change was seen in the network, coupled with increasing involvement and intervention from central government.

Following a period of temporary nationalisation during the First World War, in 1921 a new Ministry of Transport was created, one of the first tasks of which was to look at the railway system with an eye to 'creating a smaller number of great railway companies, to which should be assigned a regulated monopoly of the district in which it is situated' from the myriad of private companies currently operating the system. The proposal to create a 'Big Four' in Britain – the 'Grouping' – came to fruition in 1923, with the majority of the country's railway companies being subsumed by a larger GWR, the newly formed London Midland & Scottish Railway (LMS), the Southern Railway (SR), and the London & North Eastern Railway (LNER).

While the latter two were of little relevance to the Birmingham area, the GWR and LMS became the city's rail operators. Whereas prior to the Grouping many areas had more than one company, and in some instances stations, serving them, economies of scale now came into play, particularly in the case of the LMS, which had inherited a somewhat outdated and 'tired' fleet of locos and stock from the LNWR, and took a long hard look at where cuts could be made.

Hence, when the Second World War broke out and the railways were once again brought under central control, passenger services such as those on the Camp Hill Line ceased, never to return. The conflict placed considerable strain on the railways in general and, through the necessities of war, they failed to receive the investment they needed to cope with such considerable use. The result was that, in the aftermath of the war, the railways were run-down, locos exhausted, and stock and infrastructure damaged and no longer fit for purpose.

The post-war Attlee Government, on a wave of nationalisation, bought the railways from their respective owners and formed British Railways in 1948, taking central control over their operation. This again led to further economies of scale, as had happened during the 'Grouping' period, but while in 1923 the many companies in the region had been reduced to two, now they had been reduced to one.

However, the final nail in the coffin of the region's original rail network, exacerbated by the gradual decline in goods traffic due to increased competition from road transport, was to come in the 1960s. An audit of British Railways' accounts, instigated by Transport Minister and firm advocate of road transport Ernest Marples, concluded that 80% of the traffic was carried on just 20% of the network, with the majority of the rest operating at a loss.

'The Reshaping of British Railways' of 27 March 1963 – or the 'Beeching Report' as it became known, after the then British Railways Chairman, Dr Richard Beeching, who masterminded it – proposed that out of Britain's then 18,000 miles of railway, some 6,000 miles should be closed, with many other lines losing their passenger services and being kept open for goods traffic only; many lesser-used stations would also be closed on the lines that survived. This was to lead to wholesale decimation of the region's railways, with many lines closing altogether and others losing a significant number of stations and services.

The late 1960s and early 1970s was a bleak period for the region's railways. The whole of the GWR Snow Hill to Wolverhampton line closed, suburban stations largely became unstaffed halts infrequently served, if at all, and goods facilities closed at all locations bar Lawley Street.

Fortunately, such a state of affairs proved to be only a brief decline in the region's railways, and by the late 1970s and 1980s the benefits of passenger services were again beginning to dawn on both local and central government with the re-opening of the Redditch to Lichfield line as the 'Cross City Route' in 1978, the Snow Hill site receiving a new station in 1987 on the 'Jewellery Line', and the Midland Metro system opening during the 1990s.

While the railways will never again return to their pre-war days, particularly in relation to goods traffic, investment is now forthcoming and, with a proposed £500 million rebuild of New Street, further Midland Metro lines in the pipeline, feasibility studies for the re-opening of the Camp Hill line to passenger services and various other developments, the future of rail around Birmingham looks bright once again.

▲ New Street, past and present: a 1930 postcard showing the station with its overall roof, and a modern view of Platform 12B looking south as a lone passenger waits to board a Cross City Line service to Longbridge. *Author's collection/Author 5 November 2003*

Route 1: New Street to Longbridge and Rubery

New Street

Grid reference 407048/286640

Subject of a never-ending saga of reconstruction proposals in recent years, Birmingham New Street has in poll after poll, both locally and nationally, featured as one of the most disliked structures standing today. Originally opened as a temporary terminus of the London & Birmingham Railway in 1851, New Street station proper opened in 1854, and was used jointly by the LNWR and the Midland Railway. However, the site has undergone drastic remodelling over the past 40 years and today is unrecognisable from the days when it was fronted by the grand Queen's Hotel, entrance to the platforms was obtained from the overhead Queens Drive, and there were two train sheds, a turntable and signal boxes. Some rebuilding was prompted by a Second World War bombing raid, which partially destroyed the old LNWR side of the station, but 1960s wisdom thought it a good idea to completely redevelop the site as a subterranean affair, underneath what is now the Pallasades Shopping Centre, and with it completely sweep away all semblance of character the station once had.

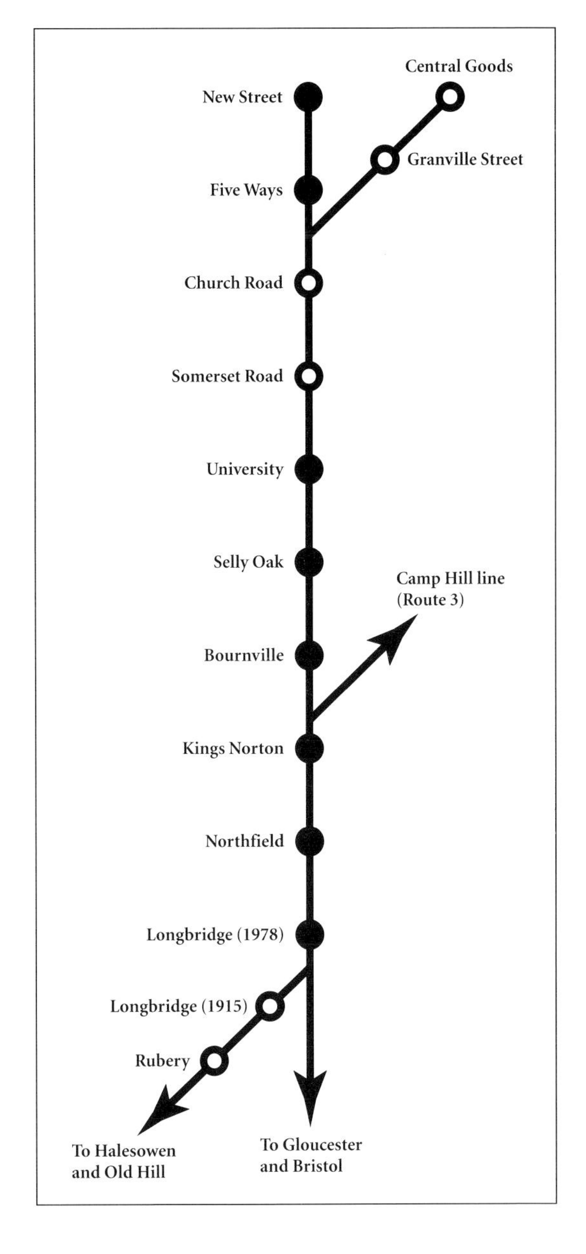

Plans have recently been submitted for a £550 million rebuild of New Street that aims to treble the size of the concourse, provide news lifts and escalators, a pedestrian 'street' and an atrium roof to 'flood the concourse with natural light'. Apparently the scheme is going to increase passenger capacity by 150%. However, one of the key issues with New Street is that all traffic travelling to and from the western end of the station passes Proof House Junction, which was never designed to handle the amount of traffic that uses it today. Furthermore, the station itself is entered through a series of tunnels, which again cannot handle the workload. These issues seem to have been somewhat overlooked by the current plans. It has also been mooted that the station may need to close during peak periods due to safety concerns. Parts of the station have been closed 15 times during 2006/07 for that reason – a very poor state of affairs for the central station of Britain's 'second city', and bad news for the 100,000 commuters who use it every day!

◀ This view of New Street station, looking down from the corner of Navigation Street and Hurst Street, shows what used to be the LNWR side to the left and the Midland side to the right, with the Pallasades Shopping Centre spanning the station above. In the foreground lies a concourse that was built in recent years as the result of safety concerns regarding fire at the station, as it lies below ground with only one route out should disaster strike. *5 September 2003*

▶ Looking west, Platforms 9 and 10 of the Midland side of the station are seen prior to demolition. In a matter of months the overall roof would be stripped away and the station remoulded in concrete. *11 April 1964; F. A. Wycherley, Roger Carpenter collection*

▶ The Midland side of the station today looks far more oppressive and grim in this shot taken from Platform 12B. On the right a Class 323 EMU is about to depart for Redditch. *5 November 2003*

▲ On the corner of Navigation Street and Brunel Street sits New Street signal box, built to replace the original signal boxes at the station, which were all decommissioned and removed with the rebuilding during the mid-1960s. *5 November 2003*

▶ This LMS timetable from 1936 shows some of the local services operating out of New Street. It is interesting to note just how many of the stations listed exist today. *Author's collection*

BIRMINGHAM (New Street) STATION—continued.

Plat. No.	TIME.	DEPARTURES—Weekdays.
	a.m.	
2	5 30	Monument Lane, Winson Green, Soho, Smethwick, Spon Lane, Oldbury, Albion, Dudley Port, Dudley, Wolverhampton.
1	6 0	Smethwick, Oldbury, Dudley Port; Dudley, Wednesbury; Tipton, Deepfields, Ettingshall Road, Wolverhampton, Four Ashes, Gailey, Penkridge, Stafford; Newport (Salop), Wellington, Shrewsbury; Stoke-on-Trent, Macclesfield, Stockport, Manchester (London Road).
1	6 1	Vauxhall, Aston, Witton, Perry Barr, Great Barr, Newton Road, Bescot, Walsall; Pleck, Darlaston, Willenhall; Bloxwich, Wyrley, Cannock, Hednesford, Rugeley (Town), Rugeley (T.V.), Colwich, Milford & Brocton; Pelsall, Brownhills, Hammerwich, Lichfield (City), Lichfield (T.V.), Alrewas, Barton & Walton; Armitage.
2	6 25	Vauxhall, Aston, Gravelly Hill, Erdington, Chester Road, Wylde Green, Sutton Coldfield, Four Oaks.
6	6 32	Five Ways, Selly Oak, Bournville, King's Norton, Northfield, Barnt Green, Alvechurch, Redditch, Studley, Coughton, Alcester, Wixford, Broom Junc.; Stratford-on-Avon; Salford Priors, Harvington, Evesham.
1	6 35	Adderley Park, Stechford, Marston Green, Hampton-in-Arden, Berkswell, Tile Hill, Coventry; Coundon Road, Foleshill, Bedworth, Chilvers Coton, Nuneaton (T.V.).
5	6 39	Camp Hill, Moseley, King's Heath, Hazelwell, Lifford, King's Norton, Northfield, Barnt Green, Blackwell, Bromsgrove, Stoke Works, Droitwich, Worcester (Shrub Hill); Great Malvern, Hereford, Bromyard, Leominster; Wadborough, Defford, Eckington, Bredon.
1 (Bay)	6 40	Vauxhall, Aston, Witton, Perry Barr, Great Barr, Bescot, Walsall; Bloxwich, Wyrley, Cannock, Hednesford.
2	6 42	Monument Lane, Winson Green, Soho, Smethwick, Spon Lane, Oldbury, Albion, Dudley Port; Dudley, Wednesbury; Tipton, Deepfields, Ettingshall Road, Wolverhampton.
4	6 48	Camp Hill, Brighton Road, Moseley, King's Heath, Hazelwell, Lifford. (Will not run Saturday, August 1st.)
5	6 55	Tamworth, Burton; Coalville; Derby; Buxton, Manchester (Central), Liverpool (Central); Loughboro', Nottingham, Mansfield, Lincoln; Sheffield; Hull via Pontefract; Barnsley; **Leeds (Wellington)**; Harrogate; Bradford (Forster Square); Carlisle; **Glasgow (St. Enoch)**; **Edinburgh (Waverley).**
2	6 55	Vauxhall, Aston, Gravelly Hill, Erdington, Chester Road, Wylde Green, Sutton Coldfield, Four Oaks.
1	6 58	Adderley Park, Stechford, Hampton-in-Arden, Coventry (Coundon Road, Foleshill).
3	7 0	(Saturdays only.) **"Isle of Man Boat Express."** Smethwick, Dudley Port, Wolverhampton, Penkridge, Stafford, Liverpool (Lime Street).
6	7 10	Five Ways, Selly Oak, Bournville, Lifford.
1	7 10	Stechford, Berkswell, Tile Hill, Coventry.

N.B.—Platform Arrangements are subject to alteration.

Granville Street

Grid reference 406257/286282

Opening in 1876, Granville Street station marked the original 'city centre' terminus of the then Midland Railway-owned Birmingham West Suburban Railway (BWSR). In reality, however, the station lay some distance from the centre of Birmingham due in part to financial constraints preventing the crossing of the barrier that was formed by the canal basin at the southern approach to the town – a situation exacerbated by the BWSR's cost-cutting approach to route planning with the line being appended to the bank of the Worcester & Birmingham Canal for much of its route.

The station itself was of purely functional construction, comprising a single wooden platform and wooden ticket office/waiting room together with a passing loop to enable locomotives to run around their trains for the return journey along the then single-track line.

The station closed just nine years after opening when, in 1887, the Midland Railway, due to increasing passenger demand, doubled the former Birmingham West Suburban line and undertook the necessary engineering works to take the railway under the canal basin at a lower level than at Granville Street, bypassing the station site to enter the LNWR/Midland joint station at New Street. The trackbed at the Granville Street station site was then extended to serve the Midland Railway's new Central Goods Station, where it remained in use until 1967.

◀ This is the site of Granville Street station, with the tunnel mouth ahead leading to the site of the Midland's Central Goods Station, and the Worcester & Birmingham Canal at the top of the embankment to the right. Some 120 years since closure, apart from the line of the trackbed itself, no discernible remains of the station have survived. The scene has also changed considerably since the days of the station with, to the left of the shot, the brick parapet marking the side of the cutting through which what is now the Cross City Line passes by on its way into New Street station. *5 September 2003*

◀ The view in the opposite direction shows the line heading off towards its connection with the Birmingham West Suburban line between what is now Five Ways station and the site of the long-gone Church Road station. The two short tunnels ahead passed under Bath Row and Bishopsgate Street, the right-hand one serving a passing loop and siding connection for goods trains waiting to enter the Central Goods facilities. Such is the reclaiming power of nature that it is hard to discern that this site is in the heart of Birmingham city centre! *5 September 2003*

Five Ways

Grid reference 406000/285905

At first glance, Five Ways station does not appear to have much of interest from a historical perspective. However, the station, which originally opened in 1885 with the New Street Extension to the BWSR, is significant for what remains at the site to indicate the history of the line itself. The station operated until 1944, when it was closed to passengers but retained as a ticketing stop for trains leaving New Street. It later fell into total disuse, only to re-open in 1978, having been rebuilt as part of the Cross City Line project.

▲ The unmistakable stylings of a Cross City Line station are seen here at Five Ways, with the original Midland station building beyond, now used as commercial premises, from which the platform was originally accessed via a rather precarious-looking wooden staircase fixed to the blue-brick side of the cutting in which the platforms sit. *5 September 2003*

▶ The station itself is fairly uninspiring, as seen in this view looking towards the tunnels that lead into New Street station, and there are no structures of historical significance still standing at track level today. Interestingly, of all the stations south of the city on the Cross City Line, Five Ways performs poorest in terms of passenger revenue; as it lies in the business district, many commuters alight here but few board trains to travel elsewhere other than those merely making the return journey from their place of work. *5 September 2003*

▲ Here we see why the Five Ways site is of historical interest. Looking south from Islington Row Middleway, with the station to our right, the platform canopies can be seen to the right of the shot, and in the middle the trackbed of the original line of the BWSR as it headed to its Granville Street terminus a short distance behind the photographer. To the left is the ever-present Worcester & Birmingham Canal. As mentioned in the introduction to this section, the original route was retained until 1967 for access to the Central Goods Station, and a walk along the old trackbed yields many relics of the line's operational days. *5 September 2003*

Church Road

Grid reference 405435/285302

Opening with the line in 1876, Church Road station, sited in the highly affluent suburb of Edgbaston, fared extremely poorly in terms of passenger numbers. It closed in 1925, and was one of only two – Somerset Road being the other – not to be re-opened with the coming of the Cross City Line, and no trace of it remains today at track level.

▲ This rare photograph, looking south, shows the station site with both its platforms, waiting room, entrance and booking hall – above and to the right of the staircase onto the platform – still in situ. The station is in a very deep cutting, with the Worcester & Birmingham Canal off to the left and the 96-metre Edgbaston Tunnel ahead. *21 April 1929; Clarence Gilbert, Roger Carpenter collection*

▶ A similar view today shows that no trace remains of the former BWSR station – although some markings are discernible on the walling above the tunnel mouth, where the footbridge was removed. *14 January 2007*

Somerset Road

Grid reference 404980/284425

Somerset Road station opened in 1876 and was, with Church Road, one of the 'forgotten' stations in the redevelopment of the BWSR as the Cross City Line during the late 1970s. Unfortunately, as with Church Road, it did not see significant passenger numbers during a time when traffic on the line was increasing, and a decision was taken in 1930 by the then operator, the LMS, to close the station.

◄ This undated photograph shows the southbound platform around the turn of the last century. While of poor quality, it is one of only two photographs I have seen of the station and is included here as it provides a valuable record of a long-gone station as a passenger service pulls in heading south from Birmingham New Street. *Roger Carpenter collection*

▼ No discernible remains of the station can be found today except for along the walling of the Somerset Road bridge. To the right of the shot can be seen the bricked-up entrance to the stairs that once led down to the southbound platform. *12 August 2003*

▶ This view from Somerset Road shows the site of the station today with the line snaking off into the distance towards the city. The platform seen in the period photograph was in the right foreground, and the BWSR's ever-present companion, the Worcester & Birmingham Canal, is out of shot behind the fence to the extreme right. *14 January 2007*

University

Grid reference 404407/283705

This is one of the two stations – the other being Longbridge – that was purpose-built for the opening of the Cross City Line south of Birmingham in 1978. As the name suggests, the station sits at the heart of the University of Birmingham campus and also the site of the sprawling Queen Elizabeth Hospital. It enjoys high passenger usage during term-times and is a stone's throw from the site of Somerset Road station. which closed in 1930.

▼ University station's booking office follows the same architectural form as the other stations on the line, with the platforms lying to the right in a deep cutting. While enjoying a flourishing trade, the majority of fares taken at this station are to Selly Oak – one station away – which serves an area of terraced housing, a considerable proportion of which has been converted into student dwellings, and to New Street, two stops away. *5 September 2003*

▲ At track level, this is the view from the Birmingham-bound platform looking south, with the booking office itself appended to the bridge ahead and just out of shot to the right. Facilities are meagre, and although there is a shop on this platform, its opening hours are sporadic, operating primarily during term-time. As there are no residential developments near the station, passenger numbers fall dramatically when the University is on vacation. *5 September 2003*

▼ A Class 323 EMU departs for Birmingham New Street. While the frequent 'Cross City' service provides the majority of traffic for the station, unlike other stations on this route Central Trains also operates services to Derby and Nottingham from here. *5 September 2003*

Selly Oak

Grid reference 404470/282665

Opened by the Midland Railway on its newly acquired Birmingham West Suburban Line, Selly Oak station originally consisted of a single wooden platform and wooden ticket office on what was then a single-track line. With the doubling of the track the station was rebuilt in a more substantial manner with accompanying goods yard, which survived, albeit in a derelict state, until the late 1970s, when the station was rebuilt for the opening of the Cross City Line, and the means of crossing from one platform to the other was changed from subway to footbridge. The station now enjoys significant commuter traffic together with considerable use by students from the nearby University of Birmingham campus and its surrounding roads.

▲ The current station is built partly on the site of the goods yard – as is the entire car park – and an interesting point to note is that the original route of the BWSR passed slightly to the right of the booking office seen in this shot, but was realigned with the building of a new bridge to carry the track over the Bristol Road when the track was doubled. *10 June 2004*

▶ By far the most interesting feature of the location is all that remains of the original 1876 BWSR bridge that crossed Bristol Road. Quite how and why it has survived is a mystery, but its days appear to be numbered, as a plan in under way to widen the A38 Bristol Road South through Selly Oak, and to facilitate such a scheme a new railway bridge is planned. In this view the current line can be seen passing behind this 'stub' as clearance work is begun to the left. The station itself is off-camera to the right. *10 June 2004*

▲ Ex-LMS 'Jubilee' 4-6-0 No 45662 *Kempenfelt* thunders through Selly Oak heading south, passing the carriage sidings alongside Heeley Road, to the right. As with the majority of suburban stations, the carriage sidings now form a car park. The main goods yard, off to the left, also now forms the main station car park and vehicular access point to the station. *9 April 1959; Roger Shenton*

▼ Standing on Platform 2 looking south, the footbridge lies ahead with the booking office on Platform 1 across the rails. *5 September 2003*

Bournville

Grid reference 405083/281063

Bournville station opened with the BWSR in 1876 as 'Stirchley Street', with a small wooden ticket office and platform. However, when the Cadbury family purchased the large 'greenfield' site adjacent to the railway to build their now world-famous chocolate factory and Bournville village for their workers, the Midland Railway realised the potential for both goods and passenger traffic on the line and the track was doubled throughout, the station itself being renamed 'Bournville & Stirchley Street' in 1887, before becoming merely 'Bournville' in 1904.

▲ The booking office on Bournville Lane is not an original building, as is apparent, but a replacement built for the opening of the Cross City Line in 1978, and occupies the site of the previous booking office, built at the time of the doubling of the track. Ahead is the low bridge carrying both the railway and the Worcester & Birmingham Canal, to the banks of which the BWSR clung throughout its route. *5 September 2003*

▶ The southbound platform is accessible from a subway that leads under the track to the booking office. This platform is unusually narrow due to the space constraints imposed by the Worcester & Birmingham Canal, the towpath of which is immediately behind the wall to the right. Directly ahead lies the site of the junction with the defunct Cadbury Works railway and exchange sidings. However, a bridge that once carried the works railway over the line to Cadbury's Waterside Wharf is still extant. *5 September 2003*

▲ In this view we are looking towards the city from Mary Vale Road bridge. The station colour scheme is purple and white to match the colours of the Cadbury factory, which can just be discerned above the trees to the top left of the photograph. The station enjoys significant commuter traffic from the surrounding suburbs of Stirchley and Bournville, as well as from visitors to the Cadbury World museum located within the factory grounds. *5 September 2003*

Kings Norton

Grid reference 404663/279588

Opened in 1849, Kings Norton is one of the oldest stations on the Cross City Line, on what was originally the Birmingham & Gloucester Railway's line from the south to Curzon Street via the Camp Hill route. With the coming of the BWSR's Kings Norton Extension in 1892 the station was expanded to three platforms, and a level crossing, which carried Station Road across the tracks, was replaced by a footbridge; a large coal and goods yard was also built, with sidings for the adjacent Triplex Works, and the station became a significant location in the region's railways.

▶ The island platform at Kings Norton is no longer in use, but the patches in the surface where once a series of waiting rooms and other facilities stood can clearly be discerned. The station once boasted frequent excursion services operating to many top seaside resorts! *14 July 2003*

▼ This view, looking south towards Northfield, shows the remains of the goods yard and, beyond that, the Triplex Works (now Pilkington Glass). A small part of the goods yard has been retained as an On-Track rail depot – their shed can just be discerned in the distance to the left of the track. In my youth there were multiple sidings here, many of which were lined with car transporter trains full of Austin cars from the nearby works at Longbridge and the satellite works off Melchett Road nearby. *14 July 2003*

▲ The remains of the original Midland Railway booking office survived multiple vandal attacks, arson and complete abandonment to appear, from the outside at least, to be in reasonable condition, albeit without part of its roof following a particularly serious arson attack. *14 July 2003*

▼ Later, and completely out of the blue, I received an email from a railway enthusiast informing me that demolition work had begun, so I grabbed my camera and raced to the station to take a series of shots. Network Rail had deemed the structure unsafe and set about turning the site into a new section of car park – something that was achieved in a remarkably swift time! *26 February 2006*

▶ The present booking office on Pershore Road South was added to the station in 1978 with the introduction of the Cross City Line. *14 July 2003*

Northfield

Grid reference 402518/278962

Northfield station is somewhat of a hybrid; whereas Longbridge is a product of the regeneration of local railways during the 1970s, Northfield is an original station (opened in 1870) that was considerably remodelled during the 1970s with new up and down platforms being added and the original island platform taken out of use.

▼ This is Northfield station's main entrance, viewed from car park. As with many suburban stations, the car park is built on the site of the original goods facilities, which once included a fixed crane for the loading and unloading of wagons. *8 July 2003*

▲ This undated postcard shows the station in Midland Railway days, looking north, with the goods sidings to the left and station staff posing for the camera. By the early 1970s the station had become an unstaffed, and infrequently served, halt, and the station building seen here had been removed and replaced by a 'bus shelter'. *Author's collection*

▼ In this view from the southbound platform, looking north, the now disused island platform is rapidly being reclaimed by nature. At the end of the platform the line crosses West Heath Road, and access to the island platform was at one time gained from a doorway in the middle of the bridge via rather gloomy stairs. *8 July 2003*

▶ This rather uninviting passage allows access to the station from Station Road; the change in the tunnel height indicates the point at which the now bricked-up entrance to the island platform is located to the right. Laid into the subway floor ahead is the date '1892', which refers to the quadrupling of the line and the associated expansion of the station site. *11 July 2003*

Longbridge (1978)

Grid reference 401390/277625

A relative latecomer to the region's railway scene, today's Longbridge was one of two stations purpose-built for the Cross City Line on the ex-BWSR route south of Birmingham. Opening in 1978, the station was built for commuters living on the southern border of the city on a site not previously occupied by a station, although the Birmingham & Gloucester Railway did open a temporary halt at Cofton, a short distance along the track, during the line's construction.

▼ It is a shame that, with the significant funds available for redevelopment of the line, a more aesthetically pleasing architecture was not employed – a blight that affected all those stations on the line south of Birmingham. The station building itself is not the only relative newcomer to this scene: this section of Longbridge Lane itself replaced the original line of the road over the railway, which today can be found still in use behind the photographer. *8 July 2003*

▲ The station itself is equally uninspiring, as can be seen in this view looking south. The land to the right, beyond the hedge, is currently occupied by the Austin Social Club, but with the demise of the MG Rover Works (which can just be discerned in the distance), it is rumoured that the club is to be demolished and a Park and Ride scheme initiated at Longbridge. The only parking currently available can be seen to the right along Tessell Lane! *8 July 2003*

▼ This shot, taken from the original Longbridge Lane bridge, shows Halesowen Junction immediately to the south of the station. To the left the Cross City Line heads off toward Barnt Green and to the right is the southern end of what was the Halesowen Railway. Immediately around the bend is the site of the Austin Works railway, and beyond that the original Longbridge station (see next page). The line is now defunct and, despite a proposal to re-open part of it to a proposed station at Frankley, with the closure of the works part of the trackbed has been lifted a few hundred yards from this spot. *8 July 2003*

Longbridge (1915)

Grid reference 400812/277538

Built in 1915, the first station to bear the name Longbridge was opened by the Midland Railway at its end of the Halesowen Railway that it jointly operated with the GWR. Sited in the heart of the Austin Motor Company works, the station catered for the thousands of workers who did not live within walking distance of the site and came by workmen's trains, which operated between here and Old Hill up until 1958 – nearly 40 years after other passenger services had ceased on the line.

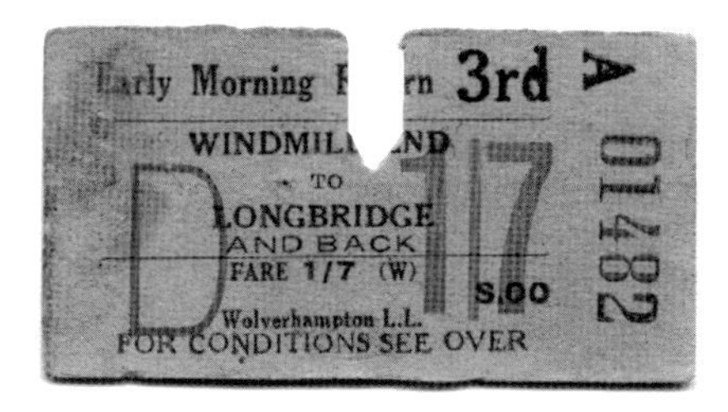

▼ It is a miracle, but for some reason the station building, built in 1936, has remained unscathed since construction, fronting Bristol Road South (A38). In fact, such is its charmed existence that it has outlived the former Austin works, which, since this photograph was taken, has closed and the parts of the factory surrounding the booking office – mostly built in 1916 – demolished! *8 July 2003*

▲ In happier times this photograph, looking towards Halesowen, shows the platforms in the heart of the works with the booking office above to the rear. Not only could the station be accessed via the booking office – which was later used for parcel despatch – but a turnstile entrance existed just out of shot to the bottom left of the photograph, still in situ today. *13 April 1951; John Edgington*

▼ Following the demolition of the West Works, it was finally possible to get a clear shot of the station site. The booking office is immediately to the left in this view, looking towards Halesowen and the site of the platforms from Bristol Road South. The track had been lifted several days before this photograph was taken, and the station footbridge, which lay just ahead and was the vantage point from which the 1951 photograph was taken, removed. *20 December 2006*

▶ The end of the line! Within the former Austin works site, this is the buffer stop marking the end of the Halesowen Railway line today. Ahead are the now lifted sidings that served the works and, beyond them, the station itself. This small piece of the railway was retained by the works as a head shunt and was, until the closure of the works and the lifting of the track between here and the station, leased by EWS. *18 November 2006*

Rubery

Grid reference 399088/278275

The former Halesowen Railway station at Rubery holds fond memories for me – although I never knew it as a functioning station, the platforms and a deserted crossing-keeper's house nearby provided a great playground for me as a child during the early 1970s. Opening in 1883 the then independent, and verging on bankrupt, Halesowen Railway envisaged Rubery station as providing significant passenger traffic, located as it was near to the popular tourist destination of the Lickey Hills to the south of Birmingham. However, fierce competition from omnibus services along the A38 to the Lickey Hills, which provided a direct service – as opposed to a half-mile walk from the station – ensured that passenger numbers were not forthcoming and, under the Midland Railway, who jointly operated the Halesowen Railway with the GWR by this time, the station was closed to passengers in 1919.

▶ A few hundred yards along the trackbed from Rubery station lies one of the few remaining relics of the Halesowen Railway. Heavily overgrown and litter-strewn, this bridge was built for farm access and, apart from the level of the trackbed being considerably raised from its running days, it is in remarkably good condition! *3 April 2003*

▲ Although closed to passengers in 1919, the station goods sidings were retained in use until 1964, as seen in this view looking towards Halesowen. The station provided the only passing loop on the single-track line, and its goods facilities saw use conveying sandstone from the adjacent Holly Bank Quarry. Interestingly, spurs from the railway were also laid at varying times to serve the construction of both Frankley Waterworks and Hollymoor Hospital, the latter operating as a field hospital during the First World War, when Rubery station, temporarily at least, saw significant passenger traffic as wounded soldiers were ferried to and from the hospital via train. However, neither 'branch' was still in situ at the time of this photograph. *11 July 1954; D. J. Norton*

▼ Standing at the site of the station building seen in the previous photograph, and looking in the same direction, we see that there are no remains of the railway here, although a rummage through Balaam's Wood to the rear of the photographer did yield a signal post mounting and gatepost in the undergrowth. During the early 1970s, what was a rural idyll was swept away for the construction of the sprawling Frankley housing estate, and with it most of the remnants of the railway including the platforms, which had survived until then in a very dilapidated state. *22 March 2006*

Route 2: New Street to Chester Road

New Street – see Route 1, page 13

Curzon Street

Grid reference 407865/287060

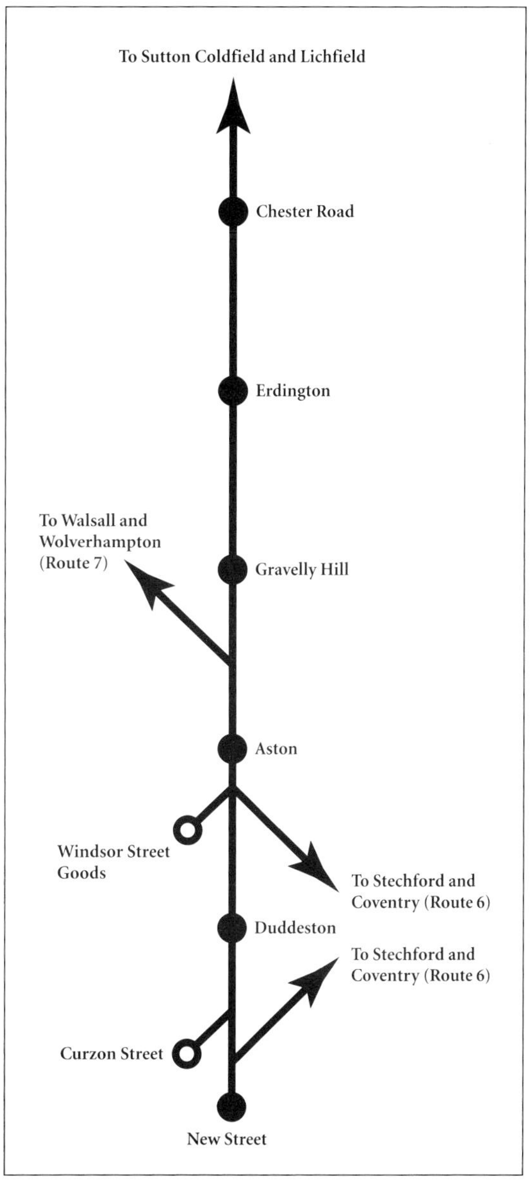

Curzon Street, or merely 'Birmingham station' as it was known until 1852, was the first town centre passenger station to be opened in Birmingham, lying at the end of what was then the London & Birmingham Railway. The station was fittingly grandiose: its classical entrance building with pillared frontage was designed in 1838 by Philip Hardwick, who also designed the original Euston station at the other end of the line. A year later the Grand Junction Railway completed its line into the town centre with the construction of an adjacent terminus at Curzon Street. However, in 1846 the GJR merged with the L&BR, together with the Manchester & Birmingham Railway, to form the London & North Western Railway. The newly formed company looked for a more central location and began work on New Street station, completing the linking of its London main line with the station in 1854. This rang the death knell for passenger services at Curzon Street, but the station was kept on as a goods facility until final closure in 1966.

▼ This Fine Art & General Insurance Company document from 1938 was drawn up for the annual insurance policy renewal at Curzon Street and provides a plan of part of the site when it was a goods-only station under the LMS. *Author's collection*

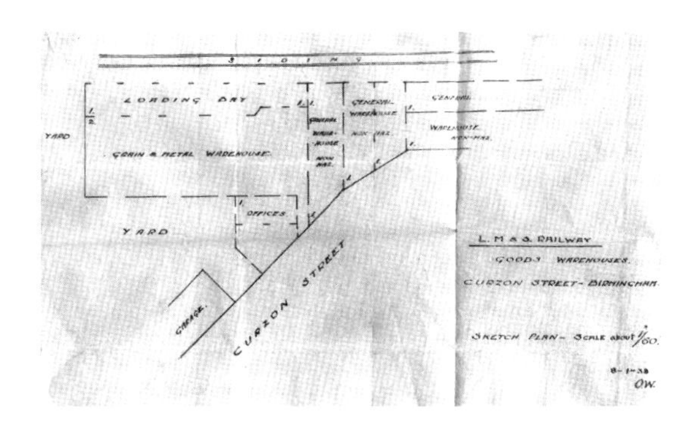

▲ Unfortunately the Curzon Street site was contained within a high wall on three sides and a railway embankment on the other, so photographs of the interior are rare. This photograph was taken from a Wolverhampton-bound express and, while not quite sharp, it gives some idea of the extent of the site; note the signal box on the right. *Kidderminster Railway Museum*

▲ While much photographed from the road side, this seldom-seen view of the station side shows the original station booking office and was only made possible due to site clearance work being undertaken. After closure as a goods station, the site became home to a Royal Mail parcels distribution centre until work for the new Eastside Development began. The building is a listed structure, and a use for it has yet to be found; apart from losing its hotel, which was an annex to this structure on the right, it is in remarkably pristine condition. *25 March 2007*

▶ In contrast to the L&BR station, the Grand Junction's station was a far more modest affair, with the station buildings themselves 'hidden' behind a façade wall that fronted on to Curzon Street itself. This photograph shows the remains of the façade wall; note the well-worn brick protecting bollards on either side of the gate. This is the only structure remaining from the GJR station and I would assume its days are numbered! *9 January 2004*

Duddeston

Grid reference 408830/287855

Originally opened as 'Vauxhall' in 1837, Duddeston station has a far from insignificant place in the history of Birmingham's railways. Phenomenally run-down and semi-derelict the station site may be today, but at one time it housed the temporary terminus of the Grand Junction Railway from Liverpool via Stafford – the first railway to reach Birmingham. When the permanent terminus opened at Curzon Street in 1839, Vauxhall became a goods-only station until rebuilt and re-opened in 1869 under the LNWR, which had absorbed the GJR in 1846. It was renamed Vauxhall & Duddeston in 1889 before finally becoming just Duddeston.

◀ Duddeston station was once a considerable railway establishment, yet today it is reduced to a single-platform, overgrown ruin. I think that more than any other operational station I have visited, Duddeston serves best to graphically illustrate the decline of Birmingham's railways. Here we see the entrance to the booking hall and station on Duddeston Mill Road. *5 September 2003*

▼ There is only one operational island platform at Duddeston today, seen here looking north. As it is the first station out of New Street to the north, the flow of traffic through it is very heavy, but stopping trains are rather infrequent and there are no facilities on the platform to indicate what trains will be arriving and when. The unkempt platform to the left is disused, and beyond it lie sidings that housed permanent way departmental stock and a brick-built engine shed, the side of which can just be discerned to the extreme left. *5 September 2003*

▲ Ex-LNWR 0-8-0 No 48930 waits to depart with an SLS special. To the left are the carriage sheds, which stood, abandoned and vandalised, until electrification of the line in the 1990s. *2 June 1962; Roger Shenton*

Aston

Grid reference 408762/289655

A shadow of its former self, Aston station opened under the newly formed LNWR in 1854 and now sits on the heavily used Cross City Line between Redditch and Lichfield. The station is located between two junctions: to the north is the junction of what is now the Cross City Line to Lichfield with the ex-GJR line to Wolverhampton, while to the south is the junction of lines serving New Street (originally Curzon Street), the ex-L&BR line to Coventry, and a spur that once served Windsor Street Goods and Gas Works. The station has undergone rebuilding in recent years and the bridge over Lichfield Road, against which the station abuts, was replaced in 1906 and has had something of a 'makeover' of its brickwork in recent times, so there is little of historical interest at the site today.

The less than inspiring entrance to the station from Lichfield Road leads to the Lichfield-bound platform. The blue brickwork here is a façade, built over the original structure when the station underwent a 'makeover' in recent years, complete with lift installation. *24 November 2004*

Here we see the 'new' bridge across Lichfield Road, to the left, contrasting with the arches of the old bridge, still partially in use. Originally the entire bridge was a series of low brick arches, but these were replaced with the current structure in 1906, not least due to the problem that they were only high enough to permit the passage of single-deck electric trams at a time when the tram (coupled with the emergence of commuter travel) was beginning to dominate the public transport scene, and greater demand required the use of double-deck trams. *24 November 2004*

▲ Looking towards the city we see the Lichfield platform building, which acts as the booking office, and the junction ahead beyond the Lichfield Road bridge parapet; the line to Coventry heads to the left and that to New Street to the right. Not the most inspirational of buildings, such waiting rooms largely appeared on the Cross City Line during electrification in the 1980s. Originally there were two significant single-storey station buildings, one on each platform, complete with canopies. *24 November 2004*

Gravelly Hill

Grid reference 410095/290850

Opened by the LNWR in 1862, Gravelly Hill station has enjoyed a fairly inauspicious life in the region's railway history. The route upon which it lay was busy, so it escaped the Beeching-era cuts, it had no goods yard to be closed, and it now forms part of the Cross City Line, which is the busiest in the region. However, the coming of the Cross City Line in the mid-1970s did encourage a 'rationalisation' of facilities – the old BR synonym for 'removal' – and a shift in platform positioning.

▼ In this view, looking towards Sutton Coldfield, the only original feature, the booking hall, can be seen on the Birmingham platform. The booking hall is entered via a walkway from Frederick Road at the top of the embankment to the extreme right, with the ticket counter on the upper level, together with the exit to the footbridge, which gives access to both platforms. The lower tier of the building today serves no purpose. *24 November 2004*

▶ This undated postcard – from the early 20th century – shows the station looking positively rural in setting, belying the fact that it is situated only some 3 miles to the north-east of Birmingham city centre. The view is looking towards Birmingham – note the position of the platforms in relation to the two-storey booking office. *Author's collection*

The second photograph shows the same view, and the striking comparison reveals that not only have the waiting rooms gone – largely to be predicted following a redevelopment of a station site – but that the platforms themselves have shifted along the track. The ends of the platforms nearest Hunton Hill bridge, from which the photographs were taken, have been cut back, and the other ends extended! Quite why this was done is not apparent. *24 November 2004*

Erdington

Grid reference 410980/292305

Erdington station also opened in 1862 on the LNWR's line from New Street to Sutton Coldfield and, after 1884, Lichfield. As with the majority of stations on what is now the Cross City Line, it has suffered the fate of 'modernisation'. However, unlike many of the other stations, at Erdington this process was more gradual, with the final removal of its period structures coming with the electrification of the line in the early 1990s and the destruction by fire of the original booking office a short time previously.

◀ The current booking office is located at the top of the ramp that gives access to the Birmingham platform from Station Road, seen here looking towards Lichfield. Not immediately discernible in this view is the only feature at the station from an earlier time, a metal 'bus shelter'-style waiting room standing just beyond the booking office. *24 November 2004*

▼ In this view, looking south from the Birmingham platform, a Class 323 EMU arrives from New Street en route to Lichfield Trent Valley, crossing the bridge over Station Road. Originally the station had wooden waiting rooms along this platform for 1st, 2nd and 3rd Class passengers, but no trace remains today. *24 November 2004*

Chester Road

Grid reference 411462/293123

Chester Road station was opened by the LNWR in 1863. As with the rest of the stations on what is now the Cross City Line, it has been stripped of all character and homogenised to be in keeping with the rest of the stations from here south to Longbridge. However, the route north from here has largely escaped such a fate!

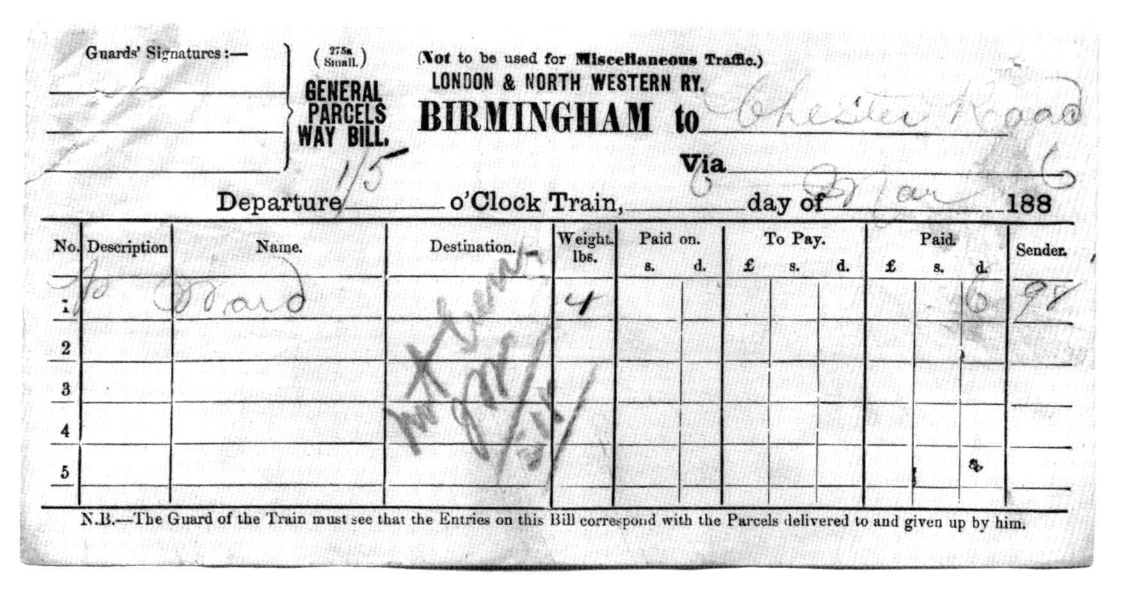

Guards' Signatures :—

(275a Small.)

GENERAL PARCELS WAY BILL.

(Not to be used for Miscellaneous Traffic.)

LONDON & NORTH WESTERN RY.

BIRMINGHAM to Chester Road

Via

Departure 1/5 o'Clock Train, 6 day of Jan 1886

No.	Description	Name.	Destination.	Weight. lbs.	Paid on. s.	d.	To Pay. £	s.	d.	Paid. £	s.	d.	Sender.
1		Road		4								6	98
2													
3													
4													
5													

N.B.—The Guard of the Train must see that the Entries on this Bill correspond with the Parcels delivered to and given up by him.

▲ A relic from a bygone era, and a bygone service: an LNWR General Parcels Waybill for a parcel travelling from New Street to Chester Road on 6 January 1886. *Author's collection*

▼ As is apparent from this photograph, the station facilities at Chester Road are non-existent bar the canopy and bench, which do little to shelter passengers from the elements. In this view looking towards Birmingham, the booking office lies ahead on the opposite platform. *14 January 2007*

▲ A Class 323 EMU pulls away from Chester Road en route to Lichfield Trent Valley. *14 January 2007*

Route 3: New Street to Kings Norton

New Street – see Route 1, page 13

Camp Hill

Grid reference 408058/284880

Opening as 'Camp Hill & Balsall Heath' in 1867, the Midland Railway's Camp Hill station, as it became in 1904, was the last northbound stop on the line before it entered the Curzon Street terminus (and later New Street). An earlier Camp Hill station, opened in 1840 by the Birmingham & Gloucester Railway, lay some quarter of a mile away, and closed prior to the opening of this station; the site was developed as Camp Hill Goods, and survived until 1966.

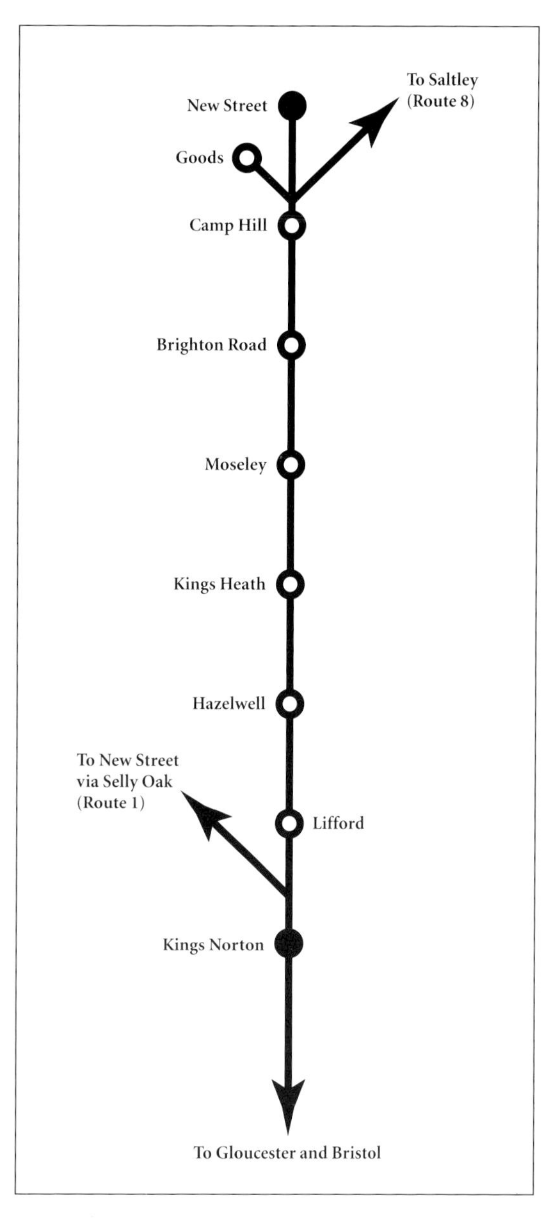

▼ Unfortunately, as with both Moseley and Brighton Road stations on this line, it is not possible to safely (or legally) gain access to the station site today. In this photograph we are standing on Ombersley Road, which would have been behind the photographer of the 1954 view overleaf. While the railway bridge is obvious, to the right of the shot a brick pillar can be seen, which marked the entrance pathway to the station site above. However, the pathway itself is now blocked by dumped rubbish, making it impassable. *12 August 2003*

▲ Camp Hill station closed in 1941, and this is the abandoned location 13 years later, looking towards the city with the grain warehouse of Camp Hill Goods visible in the centre distance. The photograph shows that by this time the platforms had been cut back and demolition workers' tools lie around the soon to be dismantled station building. *1954; D. J. Norton*

Brighton Road

Grid reference 408033/284080

Brighton Road station opened in 1875 on the Midland Railway's Camp Hill line. As with the other passenger stations on the line, it succumbed to 'wartime economy measures' in 1941 and never re-opened, and, like the others nearest to the city centre, it was located on a high embankment, rendering access impossible today.

▲ Here we see the timber-built Brighton Road station looking towards Camp Hill. Being of wooden construction, it was relatively easy to clear away once closed, although some signs did linger on into the late 1950s before final clearance took place. *10 August 1928; Clarence Gilbert, Roger Carpenter collection*

▶ This is where the Camp Hill line crosses Brighton Road itself, and is about as close as one can get to the station site. During its operational years the platform would have been visible from here, together with an entrance pathway leading to the station itself. *12 August 2003*

Moseley

Grid reference 407905/283252

This was the second incarnation of Moseley station, the first being renamed Kings Heath when the second one opened in 1867. The area it served was an affluent suburb of Birmingham and the original constructors of the line, the Birmingham & Gloucester Railway, had been pressured by local notaries, not least St Mary's Church, to the point of agreeing to provide a tunnel for a short part of the line's route so as not to spoil the landscape with a cutting!

▼ It is still possible to view the station site from Woodbridge Road – named thus as the original road bridge over the track was of wooden construction. The distinctive tunnel mouth provides a link with the postcard view opposite, but no trace of the platforms remains today. The brickwork seen to the left at track level is a retaining wall to prevent embankment slippage and is a modern addition to the scene. *9 June 2007*

▲ This undated postcard view shows the station at the turn of the last century, looking south from Woodbridge Road with the aforementioned tunnel ahead. The station, together with the line, closed to passenger services in 1941 as a 'wartime economy measure', never to reopen. *Author's collection*

Kings Heath

Grid reference 407315/282315

Opened in 1840 by the Birmingham & Gloucester Railway, Kings Heath station was originally known as Moseley until 1867 when the Midland Railway, successor to the B&GR, built a new station in Moseley village itself. Equipped with significant goods facilities, the station was the premier site on the line for traffic, but this did nothing to save it from closure, with the rest of the stations on the line, in 1941, initially as a temporary measure.

▼ This is the disused station looking towards Birmingham, with the Alcester Road crossing the line ahead. To the right can be seen two goods wagons, indicating that the yard was still in use. *16 April 1956; D. J. Norton*

▶ In the first photograph we are looking again towards the city from roughly the spot occupied by the signal box seen at the end of the platform in the 1956 photograph. Unfortunately, nothing remains today of the station or its yard; the site is now occupied by a Homebase DIY superstore and car park.

The second view is looking in the opposite direction towards Hazelwell, with a large metal fence occupying the platform site, on the other side of which is the aforementioned DIY store. Over the past two years several feasibility studies have been undertaken looking at the possibility of re-opening the now largely freight-only line for passenger services to relieve congestion along the Alcester Road, but no decision has yet been made as to whether such a scheme might come to fruition. *12 August 2003*

Hazelwell

Grid reference 406362/281357

A relative latecomer to, and short-stayer in, the region's railway scene, Hazelwell station was opened by the Midland Railway on the former B&GR Camp Hill line in 1903, becoming the last station to be built on the route. Serving the residential areas of Stirchley, Ten Acres and Kings Heath, the station was ideally situated for a growth in passenger traffic. However, this did not help to save it when the line closed to passenger services in 1941.

▲ This is the abandoned Hazelwell station looking south through Cartland Road bridge, beyond which stood the station's goods sidings and yard. The goods yard served a nearby timber merchant and was complete with a Midland signal box to control its four sidings and head shunt. *26 March 1960; D. J. Norton*

◀ We are again looking south from the station site, standing at the bottom of the entrance pathway seen on the southbound platform in the picture above. Nothing remains of the station at track level, but to the right of the shot the station house can be discerned and was, at the time of this photograph, serving as a bathroom showroom! *12 August 2003*

Lifford

Grid reference 405558/280110

The history of Lifford station is one of the trickiest in the region, there having been three stations within a stone's throw of each other all bearing the name at various times. The Birmingham & Gloucester Railway opened a short-lived station here in 1840, which closed in 1844. The BWSR then opened a station of the same name on its line, and this closed in 1885 when the third incarnation opened, once more on the ex-B&GR Camp Hill line. This station closed with the others on the route in 1941.

▲ This is Lifford station looking towards the city, with the bridge over Lifford Lane (see overleaf) behind the photographer.
1 July 1930; Clarence Gilbert, Roger Carpenter collection

▶ A similar perspective today shows that nothing remains of the final incarnation of Lifford station.
14 January 2005

▲ Viewed from the trackbed of the BWSR's Lifford line, the odd circular structure originally led up to the station on the Camp Hill line – which runs from left to right across the top of the photograph – and is one of the few remaining relics of the station. *14 January 2005*

▼ The bridge over Lifford Lane carrying the old B&GR line marks the site of the station – the entrance to the southbound side was immediately to our right, and is now occupied by Chamberlains Joinery. In the foreground another bridge, dismantled in the 1970s, carried the ex-BWSR Lifford branch over Lifford Lane to the second incarnation of the station, which stood to the left. The second station and track were retained for many years for storing wagons awaiting repair. *12 August 2003*

Route 4: New Street to Spon Lane and Rood End

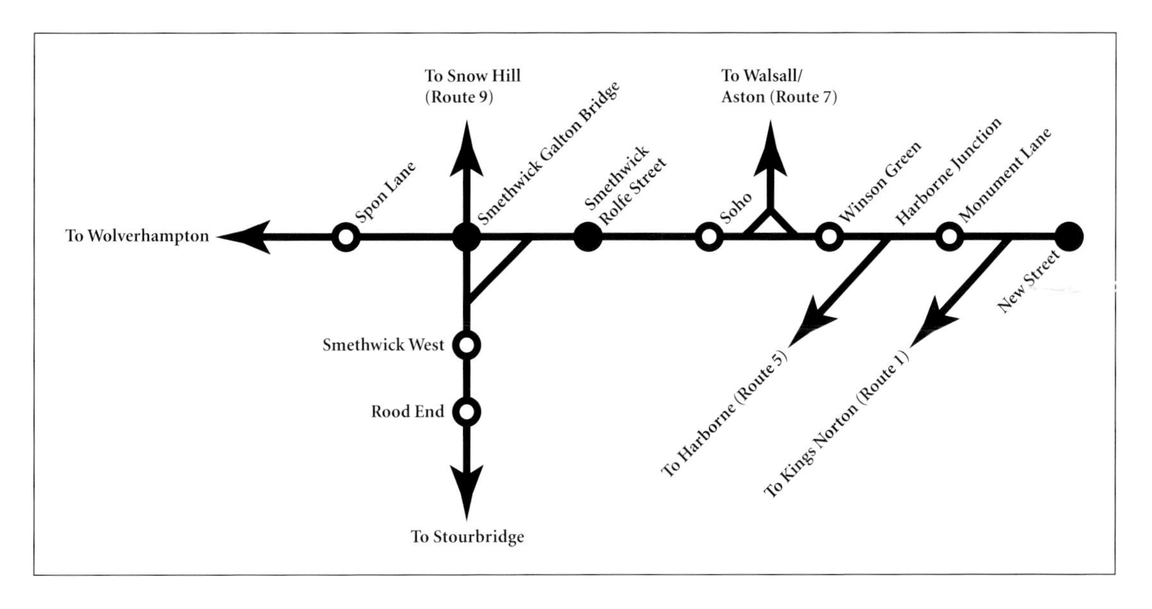

New Street – see Route 1, page 13

Monument Lane

Grid reference 405240/287138

Monument Lane station was opened by the LNWR on its New Street-Wolverhampton High Level 'Stour Valley' line in 1854, and, as well as a passenger station, facilities were also provided for a sizeable goods yard and loco shed. The station is especially interesting as it was maintained after

▶ Ex-LNWR 2-4-2T No 46757 awaits to depart with an SLS Special to travel the Harborne branch. The station booking office can be seen above the waiting rooms on Monument Lane and, directly above the second carriage of the train, the top of the signal box controlling the goods yard and shed can be seen. The signal box was set at the top of a tall tower to permit the signalman to see trains approaching from both directions without Monument Lane blocking his view. *3 June 1950; Michael Whitehouse collection*

closure to passengers as a ticketing stop, as New Street was classed as an 'open station' (access to it being a public right of way), so no ticket control was provided there. Thus stations immediately ringing New Street were used by staff to board trains and inspect and/or sell passengers tickets (Five Ways was also retained in this manner). Furthermore, the Harborne Railway joined the LNWR line at Harborne Junction, just west of the station, and its trains used to stop here on their way to New Street; thus it was also an 'honorary' fifth station on the Harborne Railway.

◀ With Monument Lane itself having been rebuilt as Ladywood Middleway, the closure of the station in 1958, and the goods facilities and shed removed, there is nothing at the site to indicate that a station was ever located here. We are looking down on the station site from Ladywood Middleway as a Virgin 'Pendolino' speeds through. *17 March 2004*

Winson Green

Grid reference 404330/287905

Opened in 1887 by the LNWR, Winson Green station lay in a deep cutting, bordered on one side by the cutting wall and on the other by Telford's Main Line canal. Closing in 1957, the site has since been completely scoured of all remnants of the station and the site at track level is now inaccessible.

▼ Looking from the Winson Green Road bridge towards the city centre, it is apparent that the track has been 'rationalised' here, and now merely comprises one up and one down line. It is, however, easy to imagine the island platform between the tracks as it is seen in the 1957 photograph opposite. *17 January 2004*

▲ Taken just five days before closure, the station is seen here looking towards Wolverhampton, with Winson Green Road crossing the line ahead by a bridge carrying the booking office at street level. *11 September 1957; David Johnson, Roger Carpenter collection*

▼ Viewed from the canal towpath, following a seemingly never-ending walk, the bridge carrying Winson Green Road is still in situ but the station has completely vanished. *17 January 2004*

Soho

Grid reference 403038/288710

Not to be confused with Soho Road, Soho station opened on the LNWR's New Street to Wolverhampton High Level line in 1867 and fared considerably less well than the other closed stations on this line (with the exception of Monmore Green), closing as early as 1949.

▲ On the last day of operation, 'Black Five' 4-6-0 No 45288 takes the 6.24pm New Street to Wolverhampton and Stoke local service out of the station for the last time. As can be seen, the station was a modest affair with the booking office sitting on the embankment on Soho Street, above and to the right of the loco. *14 May 1949; T. J. Edgington*

◀ The same scene today reveals nothing of the former station as a Class 323 EMU speeds past the spot where No 45288 stood, heading for Smethwick Rolfe Street. A total redevelopment of the area has taken place since the 1960s, rendering the surrounding area almost unrecognisable; even the road names have changed. *14 January 2004*

Smethwick Rolfe Street

Grid reference 402205/288705

This is one of only a handful of stations in the region to have undergone considerable 'rationalisation' over the years while still retaining some period character.

▲ Looking towards Birmingham from a footbridge on Great Northern Way, the station lies in the distance ahead. The white building with the pitched roof to the left of the track now occupies the site of sidings referred to overleaf. *29 December 2006*

▶ Opened by the LNWR in 1852, the booking office on Rolfe Street is a splendid example of LNWR architecture and, in terms of modernisation, has escaped largely unscathed. The interior is also 'period' to the extent that during my time with Central Trains, a colleague who staffed the booking office informed me that the IT infrastructure employed elsewhere on the network – at that time the TRIBUTE ticketing system – had not been installed here and that the cash register was just a tray! *14 January 2004*

▲ In this photograph, looking towards Rolfe Street bridge, we can see a bricked-up archway at the end of the platform that originally carried a single goods line through from sidings on the other side of the bridge to a goods yard to the right of and behind the photographer. It is also interesting to note that this end of the platform is not original but was built at the same time as the sealing-up of the arch – originally the platforms here were staggered. *14 January 2004*

Smethwick Galton Bridge

Grid reference 401390/289355

I am not one for eulogising about architecture, particularly given the state of many of the region's stations, but Smethwick Galton Bridge provides an exception to the rule. Opened in 1995, the station is on two levels, the low level catering for the Coventry-Wolverhampton line and the high level for Hereford/Stratford-upon-Avon services. Designed with a colour scheme to reflect the locally produced Ruskin Pottery, the station really is an impressive structure, as can be seen from the photographs.

▲ Standing on Telford's Galton Bridge gives the best perspective of the relationship between the low- and high-level sections of the station in the Galton Valley Conservation Area. *3 September 2003*

▶ We are on Platform 3 (of the low-level station) looking back towards the main buildings and high-level bridge. The large tower to the right is the hub of the station, giving access to all walkways and the main entrance via the system of overbridges. *3 September 2003*

◀ This is the view from Platform 1 of the high-level part of the station, looking south towards Stratford – note the use of glass in the design, and also that the line is not electrified. *3 September 2003*

Smethwick West

Grid reference 401205/289275

Smethwick West station opened in 1867 as Smethwick Junction, on the line between Stourbridge Junction and Smethwick Junction itself, where the line down to the former LNWR New Street to Wolverhampton High Level line leaves the continuation of GWR rails to join the main line between Snow Hill and Wolverhampton Low Level. The station was to close in 1995 with the opening of the prestigious Smethwick Galton Bridge, but an administrative blunder meant that the correct legal procedure for station closures was not followed, and the station had to remain open for a further year. However, in terms of service it did effectively close in 1995, since for the last year only one train per week each way ran to satisfy the 'not closed' criterion!

◀ The decrepit booking office, on Malthouse, is seen here eight years after closure of the station. Subject to a constant barrage of vandal attacks and arson, the structure has since been demolished. *January 2004; Paul Walker*

▶ Looking from the Nine Leasowes road bridge, the Smethwick Junction is ahead, with Smethwick Galton Bridge station to the left. The platforms and waiting rooms, of 'bunker' style, were still in situ on this visit to the site. *21 January 2004*

Rood End

Grid reference 400153/289053

One of the shortest-lived railway stations in the area, Rood End opened on the GWR's line from Stourbridge to the Snow Hill-Wolverhampton main line in 1867, only to close 18 years later in 1885. Today there is nothing to signify that a station ever stood at this spot, nor is there, to my knowledge, a photograph of the station from which we can discern its features (the box camera was not introduced until 1888, so it is doubtful that any photos exist).

▼ This view is from Rood End Road bridge looking towards Langley Green station, which is just round the bend ahead. The station platforms would have been in the foreground, the sidings in the distance being used as marshalling sidings for goods trains and referred to as 'Rood End sidings' or 'Rood End yard'. The area was replete with rail-connected industrial premises, so this area served as a useful point for the organisation of their traffic. In later years the sidings were used to hold tanker trains awaiting the journey along the old Oldbury route to the nearby Albright & Wilson chemical factory. *21 January 2004*

Spon Lane

Grid reference 400628/289670

Back on the former LNWR main line, another seldom-studied station in the region is Spon Lane, which opened under the LNWR in 1852 as an intermediate station on the Stour Valley Line between Birmingham New Street and Wolverhampton High Level. While outlasting many of the passenger stations on the line, the gradual erosion of stops on the route finally caught up with it in 1960.

◀ Looking towards to Wolverhampton, the lines linking with the goods yard, on the other side of Spon Lane to the rear of the photographer, can be discerned on the left. *29 June 1957; D. J. Norton*

The second photograph shows the station site, also looking west from Spon Lane. As can be seen, nothing remains of the station other than a tell-tale patch of brickwork on the bridge over the railway indicating the point at which the booking office fronted the road. Of note is the Birmingham Canal to the extreme right, and the absence of industrial premises to the left when compared with the 1957 photograph. *21 January 2004*

▲ On the other side of Spon Lane from the station site is an interesting relic that has survived the near complete clearance of the site. This gate originally led to steps down to the station's goods yard, which stood near the corner of Spon Lane and Grenville Drive and has now been removed and landscaped as parkland. A signal box was also located adjacent to the goods yard on the Birmingham side of the tracks. *21 January 2004*

Route 5: New Street to Harborne

New Street – see Route 1, page 13

Monument Lane – see Route 4, pages 59-60

Icknield Port Road

Grid reference 404400/287397

New Street

Monument Lane

To Wolverhampton (Route 4)

Icknield Port Road

Rotton Park Road

Hagley Road

Harborne

▼ Here we see the single-platform station during the 1920s, looking towards the city with Icknield Port Road ahead. The line was still in use at this time for both passenger and services and goods workings to the nearby M&B Brewery at Cape Hill and the Chad Valley toy factory at Harborne. *Michael Whitehouse collection*

Opening in 1874, Icknield Port Road station was to be the first casualty of the lack of passenger traffic on the Harborne Railway, closing in 1931, some three years before it was decided to remove the passenger services from the line altogether and operate it purely for goods services. The station also held the unenviable record as being where many passengers abandoned their train and caught a bus or tram into Birmingham along Icknield Port Road, since trains could be held here for up to 25 minutes awaiting a suitable gap in traffic on the LNWR's Stour Valley Line between Winson Green and Monument Lane stations to allow it to emerge from the branch and proceed into New Street!

▶ A similar perspective today reveals that the bridge through which the line passed under Icknield Port Road is still in situ. However, as can be seen from the angle of shot, the cutting has been filled in and the trackbed now forms a path through Summerfield Park. To the left can be seen the brick wall that lined the entrance pathway to the station, which can also be discerned in the 1920s photograph. *17 March 2004*

▼ The root of the Harborne Railway's problems! With Icknield Port Road station a few hundred yards behind the photographer, the brick pier in the foreground once carried the line over the canal to join the main line ahead into New Street, via Monument Lane. *17 March 2004*

Rotton Park Road

Grid reference 403775/286925

Also opening with the line in 1874, Rotton Park Road station featured the only passing loop on the Harborne Railway and enjoyed passenger services until 1934, when the station and line became a goods-only operation.

▲ Seen from the wooden footbridge that provided access to the site from Rotton Park Road itself in 1934, shortly before closure, this sole island platform housed a significant station building. *Michael Whitehouse collection*

◄ Today the site is in a sorry state and was part of Birmingham City Council's 'Eyesore Improvement Projects', with what had been preserved as a nature trail becoming an unauthorised refuse dump. The small overgrown 'hump' in the middle of the site signifies the site of the platform, roughly where the ground frame once stood. *17 March 2004*

▶ At the other end of the station site, with the platform to the rear, this view is looking towards the city through Selwyn Road bridge, which can be seen in the 1934 photograph. Sadly nothing remains of the station today. *17 March 2004*

Hagley Road

Grid reference 403330/286198

Hagley Road station enjoyed a longer life than the aforementioned stations at Icknield Port Road and Rotton Park Road, for although losing passenger traffic in 1934, together with the rest of the line, it survived as a goods facility until final closure in 1964.

▼ This is the site of the station today looking south towards the Hagley Road bridge and the terminus at Harborne. Interestingly, towards the right-hand corner of the shot are the remains of some station brickwork at the location of the station building seen in the postcard view overleaf, obscured by the undergrowth. *17 January 2004*

▲ This postcard view shows the station in happier times; the view is from the Hagley Road overbridge looking towards the city, and illustrates well the single-track nature of the line. Just beyond the station the goods sidings off Station Avenue can be discerned. *Circa 1913/14; Mike Musson collection*

▼ This is a similar view of the station site from the mouth of the Hagley Road bridge, with the entrance pathway above and to the left. The fact that the line is still accessible is due to it being preserved as far as Icknield Port Road as the Harborne Nature Walk. *17 March 2004*

Harborne

Grid reference 403450/284748

Harborne station opened as the terminus of the 3½-mile line built in 1874 to serve the leafy suburb. The original promoters of the Harborne Railway had seen the growing suburb as providing suitably increasing commuter traffic to justify the funding of the project, which, unfortunately, never materialised, for a number of reasons, some of which beyond their control. Hence the station, as a passenger facility, led a rather short life, and in 1934 the LMS decided that it was not economically viable to keep it open.

▲ Closure to passenger services did not mean the end of Harborne station, as it lived on until 1963 for goods purposes, with the station building itself being leased to the nearby Chad Valley toy factory as a carpentry workshop and wood store! *1971; Charles Steele*

▶ Other than 'Station Road', nothing remains today at the exact site of the station to indicate its former existence, as a development of flats now occupies the plot. However, a minute's walk from the site of the station entrance reveals this bridge over Park Road, which was restored and forms the beginning of the Harborne Walkway, which follows the trackbed as far as Icknield Port Road. The station site is immediately to the left of the bridge. *1 July 2003*

Route 6: New Street to Birmingham International

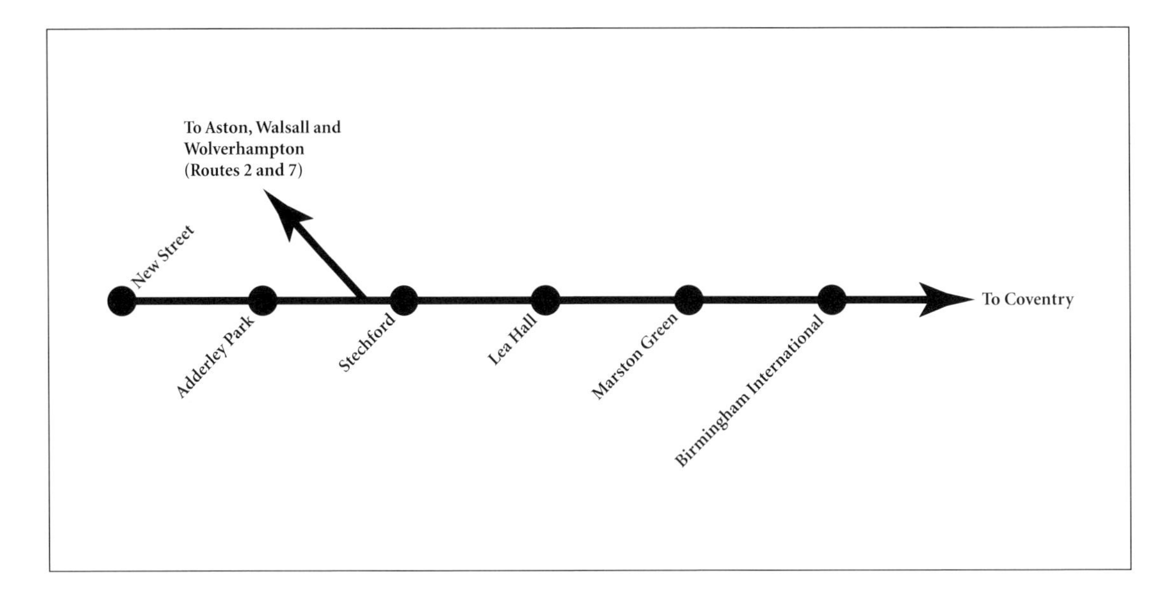

New Street – see Route 1, page 13

Adderley Park

Grid reference 409935/287252

Adderley Park was opened in 1860 by the LNWR as the first station out of the newly built New Street station on its route through Coventry to London Euston. As is immediately discernible from the photographs on this page, the station has undergone considerable 'remodelling' in the ensuing years and is both devoid of character – as are so many of the 1970s/'80s-built station buildings – and poorly kept, with graffiti and litter in abundance.

◀ The station building lies on Bordesley Green Road with the platforms lying in a deep cutting to the right of the photograph. The original booking office also lay in the cutting on the Coventry platform, but has since been removed. *6 January 2004*

▶ Looking down from Bordesley Green Road towards Coventry we get our first glimpse of this 'gateway' station – a station that greets visitors to the city as they approach New Street! From a historical perspective, of note here is the grassy corridor to the right of the cutting, which once housed the branch leading to the goods facilities on the other side of Bordesley Green Road to the rear of the photographer, the closure of which also led to the removal of a signal box that stood just past the waiting room on the Birmingham platform. *6 January 2004*

▶ Further gloom abounds as we look towards New Street with the site of the now-lifted goods sidings ahead. The most striking thing about the station is the bluish glow that encompasses the site due to the sunlight bouncing from the engineering brick walls of the cutting, which does nothing to lift the station's depressing aura. Worthy of note is the station's role as a 'ticketing station' for many years; as New Street station was at one time a public right of way, tickets were issued and checked at a ring of stations immediately surrounding it. *12 January 2007*

Stechford

Grid reference 412915/287490

Stechford station was opened in 1844 by the London & Birmingham Railway on the eve of the company's 1846 merger with the Grand Junction and the Birmingham & Manchester Railways to form the London & North Western Railway.

▶ The current station building on Frederick Road follows the 'fallout shelter' approach to station building, and is a sad replacement for the original station building, which sat astride the centre lines on the Station Road overbridge. From this entrance there is a steep staircase down the side of the embankment, the bottom of which puts you on the lifted trackbed of the relief lines. *6 January 2004*

▲ This view of Stechford station is from the Birmingham platform looking back at the Station Road bridge with the entrance pathway just beyond the 'bus shelter' on the right-hand side. It is apparent that the width of the site far exceeds its current usage indicating that some 'rationalisation' has taken place over the years, including the removal of the goods and down relief lines on the right-hand side, which connected with the goods yard on the other side of the bridge ahead. *6 January 2004*

▼ The line branching off to the right leads to Aston and is used primarily for diversionary purposes; the main line to the left continues via Adderley Park to Birmingham New Street. *6 January 2004*

Lea Hall

Grid reference 414568/287000

Opened in 1939 by the LMS, Lea Hall station is, at least architecturally, something of a curiosity in the region's railway scene. However, its semi-Art Deco stylings have done little to inspire the local youth, as the station sits on one of the most frequently vandalised stretches of railway in the region!

▶ This is the garishly painted, and heavily fortified, entrance to Lea Hall station off Lea Hall Road. The station has changed little since its opening. *6 January 2004*

▼ While the canopies give a nod in the direction of 1930s architecture, the station is also a good example of how, over a 60-year period, the time and money expended on providing aesthetically pleasing railway structures had significantly diminished to the level of the purely functional form we see here. *6 January 2004*

Marston Green

Grid reference 416678/285518

Opened by the LNWR in 1844, Marston Green unfortunately went through considerable 'restructuring' in the early 1970s following electrification of the line and has, as a result, lost all of its period features (and signal box).

◀ The booking office is off Holly Lane, a bland duplicate of other 1970s stations in the region. *6 January 2004*

▼ This view, looking towards Birmingham, is taken from the footbridge built to span the entire railway and linking Station Road with Elmdon Road, off camera to right and left respectively. Originally a level crossing stood at this spot, but was replaced during the restructuring of the site in the 1970s. *6 January 2004*

Birmingham International

Grid reference 418760/283690

With a sweeping mood of rail travel optimism growing during the mid-1970s – the Cross City Line was already in the planning stages – British Rail opened the grandiosely named Birmingham International station in 1976 to serve the needs of the rapidly expanding Elmdon Airport (now Birmingham International) and to cater for the soon-to-be-built National Exhibition Centre. The former LNWR New Street to Euston line provided the perfect solution to transport concerns at the Bickenhill site, and the station was built to serve both suburban and inter-city services.

▶ The impressive frontage of the now Virgin-operated station, on Station Way. *6 January 2004*

▼ Unfortunately, as with most new stations, what the designers give with one hand – a new station – they take away with the other – abhorrent architecture! This is a large station with platform facilities as well as a bar/cafe in the waiting area above. However, it does have somewhat of a 'New Street' feel to it, which is unfortunate; built in the middle of nowhere with an abundance of land to spare, they still had to stack floors above the platforms, making them dark and depressing. *6 January 2004*

▲ A Class 323 EMU departs from platform 5 in this view looking towards Coventry. *6 January 2004*

Route 7:
New Street to Newton Road and the Soho Loop

New Street – see Route 1, page 13

Duddeston – see Route 2, pages 40-41

Aston – see Route 2, pages 42-43

Witton

Grid reference 407985/290490

Opening in two phases under the LNWR, for passengers in 1876 and goods in 1887, Witton station sits on the busy commuter route between Birmingham New Street and Walsall, enjoying considerable rush-hour traffic as well as match-day traffic in the evenings and at weekends due to its close proximity to Aston Villa Football Club.

▼ The view from the Birmingham platform looking towards Perry Barr and Walsall reveals that there is little of significant interest other than the booking office in existence at the station. Ahead, the bridge carrying the railway over Witton Road can be discerned. *14 July 2004*

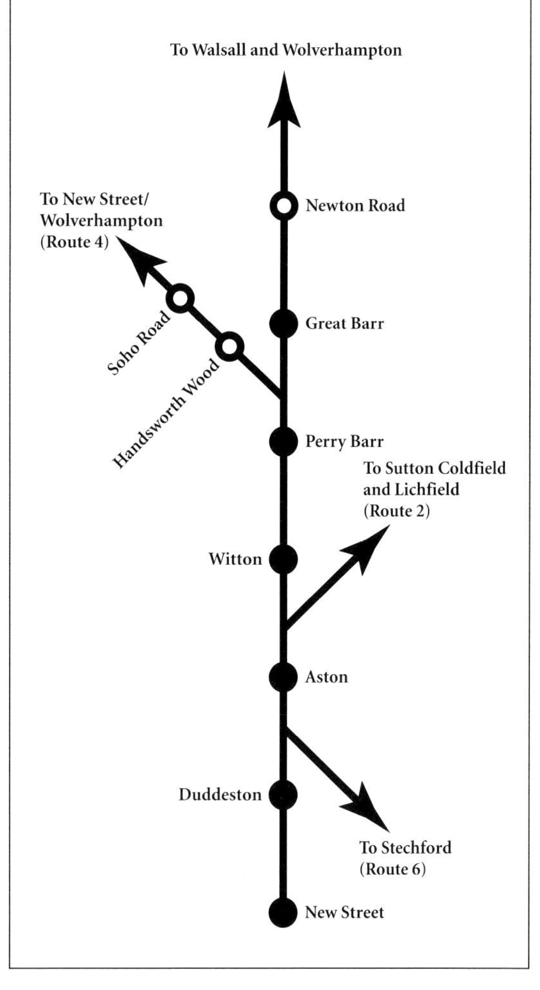

Perry Barr

Grid reference 406715/290950

Being one of the original Grand Junction Railway stations that opened with the line in 1837, my visit to the site was much anticipated. However, despite such an auspicious pedigree the architects of inner-city areas during the 1960s seem to have gone out of their way to make this one of the most aesthetically unpleasant stations in the region.

◄ The entrance to the station and booking office, the latter located to the left through the doorway, is unobtrusive in the middle of a row of concrete, prefab-constructed shops on Birchfield Road, which are showing their relatively new age considerably more than many of the 19th-century station buildings in the region. *14 July 2004*

▼ With the booking office behind the photographer, this uninspiring view greets travellers as they descend to the Birmingham platform. The original features at track level are meagre, but the overall appearance of the station is more welcoming, with the booking office above on Birchfield Road and covered stairwells descending to the platforms. *14 July 2004*

Handsworth Wood

Grid reference 405405/290450

Handsworth Wood station opened in 1896, eight years after the short line on which it stood was built by the LNWR to link its New Street to Wolverhampton High Level with its New Street to Walsall lines. Like the other station on the line, Soho Road, Handsworth Wood closed in 1941 during the Second World War, never to re-open. However, unlike Soho Road, clues to its existence can still be found at the site.

▲ This photograph taken shows the station looking towards Soho Road in what was a semi-rural and affluent Birmingham suburb, lying, as it did, in the picturesque setting of Handsworth Park. The station lay in a deep cutting between a short tunnel under Hamstead Road and the bridging of the tracks by Handsworth Park, behind the photographer. *29 June 1929; Clarence Gilbert, Kidderminster Railway Museum*

▶ A similar view in 2006 shows that nothing remains of the station at track level. Such is the location of the site that access is not possible to view it at track level today. *30 October 2006; Paul Baxter*

◀ On Hamstead Road, immediately to the right of the large section of red brick wall ahead, is a now-padlocked gate securing the entrance to the pathway down to the platform for trains heading for the New Street/ Wolverhampton High Level line. *14 July 2004*

Soho Road

Grid reference 405013/289292

Opening in 1889 under the LNWR, on a stretch of line primarily laid with colliery traffic in mind, Soho Road station was never successful with passenger traffic, being served by sporadic services from New Street via Aston and back to New Street, with even fewer services, stopping frequently, from Walsall and Wolverhampton High Level. The station was finally closed by the LMS in 1941 during the Second World War, never to re-open.

▼ Soho Road is one of the few stations that failed to ignite the interest of local railway photographers when open, and scant evidence exists today at the site to attest to its existence. Here we see the view from Soho Road – the dark patch of brickwork in the centre of the bridge marks the spot where the booking office once fronted the road. *17 March 2004*

▲ This view shows the long-derelict booking office on the Soho Road bridge, the platform already removed, looking in the direction of Handsworth Wood. The station had meagre facilities and consisted of a single island platform, remains of which can be seen in the foreground as clearance work gets under way. *1 June 1962; D. J. Norton*

▼ It is extremely difficult to view the site from track level today as there is no direct access, but as this 2006 shot shows there is nothing to indicate that a station ever existed here other than the tell-tale patch of brickwork on the Soho Road bridge. *30 October 2006; Paul Baxter*

Great Barr

Grid reference 404985/292490

Back on the former Grand Junction Railway line, Great Barr opened in 1862 as Hamstead station, and has not only undergone a name change in the intervening years but has also moved location a hundred yards or so along the line – moving from one side of Old Walsall Road to its present site. Unfortunately, as with many stations over the past 50 years, the station has also lost its goods sidings, which also lay on the other side of Old Walsall Road bridge.

▲ This is Great Barr station looking towards Walsall, showing Old Walsall Road bridge and the original station and goods yard site beyond. The long-closed Hamstead Colliery stood a short distance away and was served by a branch that led to the goods sidings being filled with coal wagons awaiting pick-up by main-line locomotives for distribution. *14 July 2004*

◀ Here we see the only structure of note at the station, the waiting room and booking office on the Birmingham platform. The structure dates from the opening of the station at this location and provides some interest at what would otherwise be a characterless site void of any passenger facilities and items of historical interest. *14 July 2004*

Newton Road

Grid reference 402272/294008

Newton Road station had three incarnations before its then owner, the LMS, decided that following the Second World War it was not worth keeping open. As one of the original Grand Junction Railway stations, it opened in 1837. However, under the LNWR it was deemed that a more suitable site should be found and in 1863 the station shifted location a short distance along the track to the junction of Ray Hall Lane. However, this move yielded few dividends in passenger numbers, so the station was shifted back to its near original position on Newton Road in 1902, where it stayed until final closure in 1945.

▲ The third incarnation of Newton Road station is seen here looking towards Great Barr, with Newton Road to the rear of the photographer. As can be seen, the station was of wooden construction and, with the redevelopment of Newton Road as a dual carriageway following closure, all traces have been swept away today. *5 August 1930; Kidderminster Railway Museum*

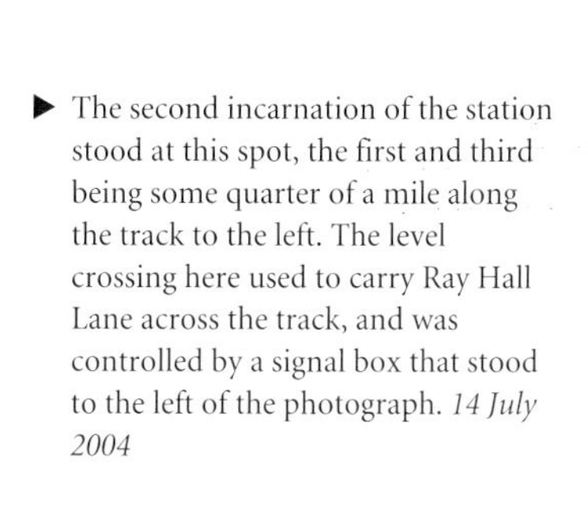

▶ The second incarnation of the station stood at this spot, the first and third being some quarter of a mile along the track to the left. The level crossing here used to carry Ray Hall Lane across the track, and was controlled by a signal box that stood to the left of the photograph. *14 July 2004*

Route 8: New Street to Castle Bromwich and Penns

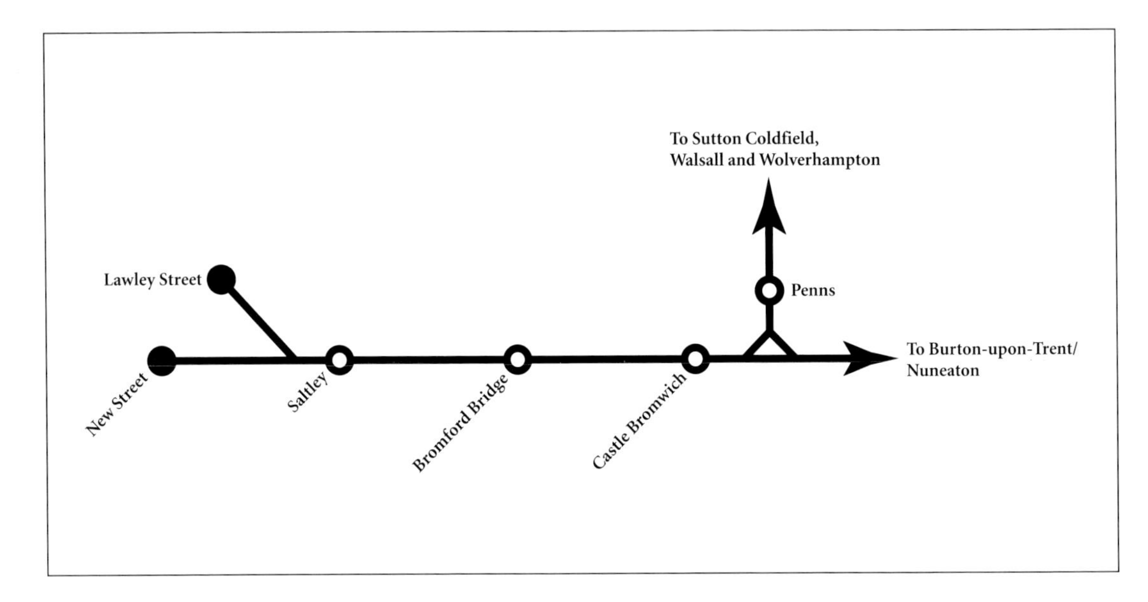

New Street – see Route 1, page 13

Lawley Street

Grid reference 408515/287065

Just two years after the Birmingham & Derby Junction Railway reached the centre of Birmingham with a line terminating at a new station at Lawley Street, the Midland Railway

◀ This view of Lawley Street is facing Birmingham New Street and shows an overhead crane to the left, an ex-Midland Railway signal box in the centre, and goods warehouse in the distance. The original passenger station building stood to the right of the line at this spot. *30 September 1967; Bob Essery*

absorbed the company and Lawley Street was bypassed with a new line into New Street in 1851, thus ending its short career as a passenger station. However, it then entered a period of significant growth as a goods facility and still remains so today.

▲ Unfortunately, it is nigh-on impossible to get a good vantage point to see inside the facilities at Lawley Street today. This view, taken from Landor Street, shows the overhead cranes that now move up and down the line transferring freight from rail to road and vice versa. *9 January 2004*

▼ The only relic discernible from the roadside is this structure on Landor Street, facing the entrance to the Freightliner depot, which dates from at least 1893 as it appears on the OS map of that year. The architectural style is that of a stabling block for horses, which were used extensively for shunting duties, even into British Railways days until 1964. *9 January 2004*

Saltley

Grid reference 409290/288345

In railway history and folklore Saltley comes out top in the area covered by this book –goods facilities, extensive workshops, roundhouse sheds, large rail-connected gas works and a station all once occupied this considerable site. Nowadays, however, none survive and the site is just a barren industrial wasteland with new factory units where once the railway dominated the landscape. Opened in 1854 by the Midland Railway, the station enjoyed a long service until closure in 1968, and consisted of a single island platform with waiting rooms and goods facilities.

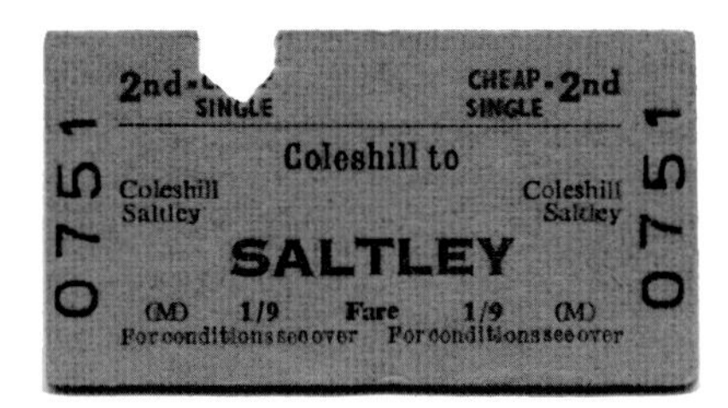

▲ In this view, looking towards Washwood Heath, the station is deserted. Off to the right stood the sprawling Birmingham Railway Carriage & Wagon works, while to the left stood a steel tube mill. *25 October 1964; Bob Essery*

◀ Today the site is a far cry from its industrial past. Looking down on the station site from Saltley Viaduct, from which it was entered, nothing remains of the station or the railway works beyond. This site is steeped in history but there is little evidence of that history today, which is a great pity. *9 January 2004*

Bromford Bridge

Grid reference 411618/289715

Opened by the Midland Railway in 1896, Bromford Bridge station's purpose was to serve special trains that arrived there on race day carrying visitors to the nearby Birmingham Racecourse, which had opened in 1865. So dedicated was the station to this traffic that when the racecourse ran its last race in 1965, the station closed too.

▲ 'Jubilee' Class 4-6-0 No 45668 passes through Bromford Bridge with a down mineral train. The photograph was taken from Bromford Bridge – note the signal box to the right, on the Birmingham platform. *5 September 1962; Kidderminster Railway Museum*

▶ Because Bromford Lane now includes a traffic island at the site of the station, a comparative view today yields poor dividends. However, standing on the other side of the traffic island from the original Bromford Lane bridge, roughly at the spot where the signal box stood, shows that nothing of the station remains, or the means by which passengers once reached platform level. *9 June 2007*

Castle Bromwich

Grid reference 413902/290400

Castle Bromwich station opened in 1842 on the Birmingham & Derby Junction Railway's line from Lawley Street through Tamworth to Derby. Enjoying a fairly inauspicious history on the outskirts of Birmingham, the station was rebuilt in 1901 by the Midland Railway, and closed in the Beeching era in 1968; the buildings were demolished during 1975.

▲ Kirtley 2-4-0 No 89A is at the head of the 12.36pm train from Walsall via Penns at the original Castle Bromwich station; the coaches are six-wheelers. The 1901 rebuilding of the station saw a new booking office mounted on Chester Road bridge, and brick waiting rooms on each platform with angular flat roofs projecting over the platforms (akin to those at Lea Hall). *1898; Roy Burrows collection*

◄ This is the scene today looking in the same direction from Chester Road bridge, which in itself is not original, the first bridge being behind the photographer. With the exception of the surviving Derby/Walsall platform on the left, nothing remains of the station. *9 June 2007*

Penns

Grid reference 413500/293397

Penns station opened in 1879 as the first station on what was then the Midland Railway's Walsall and Water Orton Branch. It closed, together with the others on the line (apart from Sutton Town, which had closed previously), in 1965, although the line was retained for goods use, a purpose that it still performs today.

▲ A tranquil Penns station is seen here during the 1930s, looking from Penns Lane bridge towards Sutton Coldfield (Sutton Town station). Ahead can be seen the bridge carrying Penns Lake Road over the tracks. *Lens of Sutton*

▶ No trace of the station buildings remains today, although a platform can clearly be seen, albeit somewhat cut back from the track. *24 March 2004*

Route 9: Snow Hill to West Bromwich

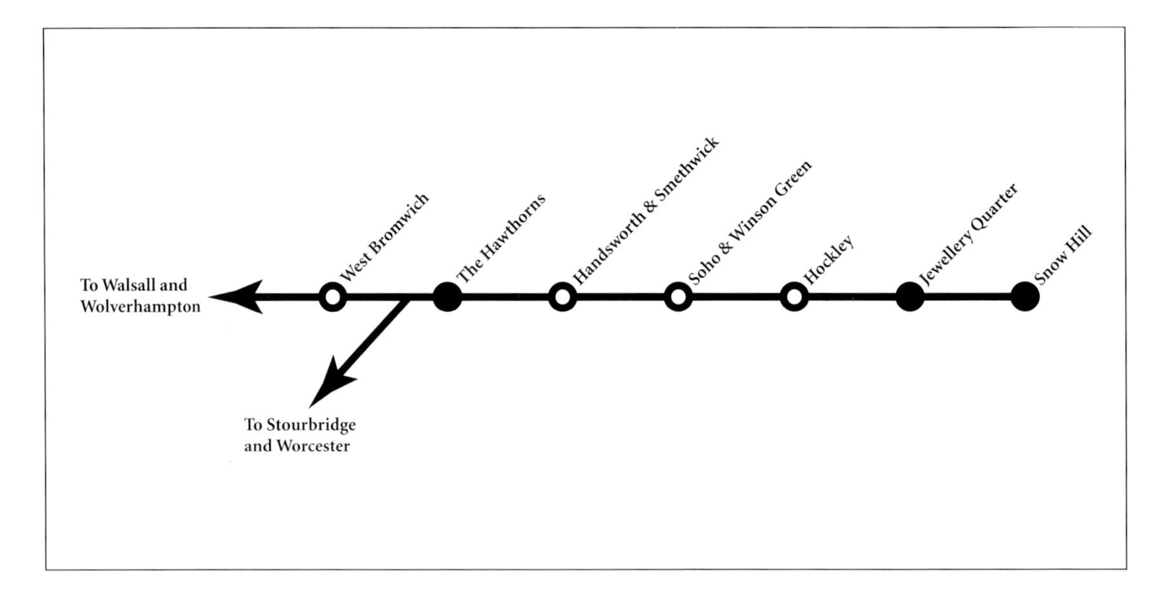

Snow Hill

Grid reference 406985/287240

With its LNWR/MR counterpart at New Street, the Great Western Railway's Snow Hill was one of Birmingham's 'big two' stations. Originally of temporary wooden construction, Snow Hill opened in 1852, giving the GWR, and Brunel's 7ft 0¼in broad gauge track, a presence in the industrialised heart of the Midlands. Rebuilt in 1871 and again in 1906, the station came to reflect the height of GWR opulence with its grand Great Western Hotel frontage, mosaic floors in the platform tea rooms and a vast subterranean booking hall and goods/parcels office – immaculately covered with white salt-glazed tiles.

Unfortunately, in 1972 British Rail decided that the Birmingham-Wolverhampton route most worthy of investment, and subsequent electrification, was New Street to Wolverhampton High Level, leaving Snow Hill rather superfluous to requirements. In addition to this, maintenance was becoming prohibitively expensive (which was somewhat accelerated by the complete neglect the station had faced since the mid-to-late-1960s when the Beeching Report indicated that the station's days should be numbered) – for example, the station was slowly creeping down Snow Hill! Thus it bowed to the inevitable and closed in 1972, together with the line up to and including Wolverhampton Low Level and the tunnel connection through to Moor Street.

▲ This undated postcard shows the sheer scale of the Great Western Hotel with the station itself accessible through the archway located in the centre. This view of Colmore Row also provides an interesting perspective as the station can be seen stretching away into the distance along Livery Street to the left. *Author's collection*

▼ Snow Hill's days are numbered and services are dwindling, the great station eventually just accommodating a Class 122 'bubblecar' shuttle service to Wolverhampton as possibly the largest 'unstaffed halt' on the rail network. Here we are looking at the deserted station towards the tunnel through to Moor Street. From March 1967 the entrances from Snow Hill, Livery Street and Colmore Row had already been closed and express services switched to New Street. *8 August 1967; D. Bathurst*

◀ Following closure of the station, the site became a car park while the station structures themselves were gradually demolished and cleared. In this photograph we are looking towards Wolverhampton with the lines lifted and the station poised for the bulldozers in 1976. With the site finally cleared by the late 1970s, bar the platforms, a rare occurrence took place: plans emerged to build a new station on the site! *Roy Dillon*

▼ Marking the winding down of this former main-line station, this timetable shows only the shuttle service to Wolverhampton and Langley Green; none of the stations listed exist today. *Author's collection*

BIRMINGHAM SNOW HILL to LANGLEY GREEN
and WOLVERHAMPTON L.L.
WEEKDAYS ONLY
from
4th MARCH, 1968
until further notice

	BIRMINGHAM S.H.	HOCKLEY	WINSON GREEN	HANDSWORTH	SMETHWICK WEST	LANGLEY GREEN	WEST BROMWICH
2	06.30	06.32	06.34	06.37	06.42	06.45	-
	06.50	06.52	06.55	06.58	-	-	07.03
2	07.14	-	-	07.18	07.23	07.26	-
	07.32	07.34	07.37	07.40	-	-	07.45
	08.13	08.15	08.18	08.21	-	-	08.26
SO	12.40	12.42	12.45	12.48	-	-	12.53
	16.25	16.27	16.30	16.33	-	-	16.38
2	16.59	17.01	17.03	17.06	17.11	17.14	-
	17.08	-	-	17.12	-	-	17.17
2	17.38	17.40	17.42	17.45	17.50	17.53	-
	17.48	17.50	17.53	17.56	-	-	18.01

◀ In 1987 the new Snow Hill was opened, originally only connected to the North Warwickshire Line via the tunnel to Moor Street. The entrance to the new station is not nearly so grand, but with the opening of the Jewellery Line in 1995, and the Midland Metro in 1999, Snow Hill became a major railway station once again – albeit somewhat scaled-down from the grandeur of its GWR heyday! *5 November 2003*

▲ The architects of the new Snow Hill paid little attention to the antecedents of the site, and, imitating the New Street model, decided upon part-burying the station under a multi-storey car park. In this view we are looking towards Moor Street with the station now comprising two island platforms. The blue railings to the left separate the Midland Metro platform (on the extreme left) from the rest of the 'heavy rail' station site. *5 November 2003*

▼ We are now looking in the opposite direction towards what was Hockley station and Hockley Goods on the line to Wolverhampton. The catenary for the Midland Metro can be seen to the right, and between here and the bridge in the distance is St Paul's Metro stop, which occupies land previously housing a turntable and sidings. *5 November 2003*

▲ Yielding much more of interest than the current station, a walk around the perimeter of the vast site yields many interesting relics from GWR days. This view shows the scale of the engineering works necessary to construct the station on its brick-built viaduct. Here we see the huge archway that carried the station over the Birmingham & Fazeley Canal in Livery Street. *5 November 2003*

◀ Again on Livery Street, a nod to the past glory of the site is this preserved doorway and section of walling – note the GWR insignia to the right and left of the structure. *5 November 2003*

Jewellery Quarter

Grid reference 405940/287985

Jewellery Quarter station opened in 1995, together with The Hawthorns and Smethwick Galton Bridge, on what was named the 'Jewellery Line', which was intended to create 'a third cross-city line linking the lines to Worcester and Hereford with those to Stratford-upon-Avon and Leamington Spa', according to Centro. The Midland Metro stop was added with the opening of that system in 1999, utilising the old Snow Hill to Wolverhampton line as far as Priestfield. The station occupies the site of some of the former Hockley goods facilities and is 100 yards or so from the site of the old Hockley passenger station.

▶ The entrance building to the station, together with the rest of its construction, is like a somewhat scaled-down Smethwick Galton Bridge in design. The station is a joint light/heavy rail stop, serving both the Leamington-Kidderminster (via Snow Hill) line and Line 1 of the Midland Metro. *17 March 2004*

▼ This is the Metro side of the station, viewed from the Wolverhampton platform, looking back towards the tunnel as T69 tramcar 08 pulls away to pass under Vyse Street en route to Snow Hill. *17 March 2004*

▲ This is a good angle to see into the Vyse Street tunnel, after which a succession of 'tunnels' (in reality wide bridges) lead the Metro line to St Paul's and the main line into Snow Hill. As far as Midland Metro stops go, this is by far the most interesting, which is of course due to the main-line route, leading to the provision of a quality structure. *17 March 2004*

Hockley

Grid reference 405698/288073

One of the saddest losses to the rail scene has been the decimation of goods facilities, felt not least at Hockley. The passenger station was a fairly modest affair (at least by GWR standards), accessed via an entrance below track level on Icknield Street. In the years since closure, Icknield Street has undergone major redevelopment and the station site was completely cleared during the late 1990s in anticipation of the Midland Metro; thus little, if anything, remains. The goods facilities at Hockley closed in 1971, but a lot more of these remain today.

▲ Seen here from All Saints Street looking towards the city, the small station can be seen to the left of the shot, dwarfed by the goods facilities that occupied the majority of the site and are seen here in disuse immediately upon closure. *1971; Frank Jennings*

▶ Today the site carries the lines of the Midland Metro (left) and the Jewellery Line (right), as seen in this view from All Saints Road bridge – the distinctive Post Office Tower in the distance links the scene with the 1971 photograph. To the right, where once the loading/unloading bays once stood, is now an industrial park, occupied largely by BT. The now residential area to the left also once housed significant facilities including an overhead crane. *17 March 2004*

▲ Not long before closure the island platform is already redundant and decaying in this shot looking towards All Saints Road. One of the soon-to-be-lifted lines here was goods-only and led to the goods sidings that once stood at Soho & Winson Green, the next stop on the line. Additionally, the site featured a wagon lift that brought goods wagons up from track level to the site of various warehousing facilities (some of which remain today). *August 1969; Roger Shenton*

▼ One of the many remains of the warehousing at the site can be seen at the junction of Pitsford Street and Icknield Street. Sadly, the top section of the warehouse was removed together with the remodelling of the site in anticipation of the return of rail services and improvements to the inner ring road; however, it had survived until the late 1980s with 'Hockley Goods' proudly painted along its side. *17 March 2004*

Soho & Winson Green

Grid reference 404762/288782

Soho & Winson Green station was opened as plain 'Soho' by the GWR in 1854 and was a typically large affair with multiple platforms, waiting rooms and trademark GWR canopies with darted valancing – very reminiscent of the GWR station at Tyseley.

▲ In its last days the station looks extremely run-down and derelict. We are looking towards Wolverhampton, and the road bridge beyond the footbridge is Benson Road, on the other side of which was the large goods yard that was also served by a goods-only line from Hockley Goods. The booking office can be seen to the right. *8 August 1969; Roger Shenton*

▶ The site today has been totally cleared and is now occupied by the Soho Benson Road Midland Metro stop, while the Jewellery Line between Kidderminster and Leamington Spa (via Snow Hill) passes through on the right, but has no stopping facilities here. To the extreme right of this view, looking towards Hockley and Snow Hill, once lay long-lifted sidings. *17 March 2004*

Handsworth & Smethwick

Grid reference 403370/289332

The one-time grand GWR Handsworth & Smethwick station opened in 1854 on the Snow Hill to Wolverhampton Low Level line, and boasted goods sidings, two up and two down running lines, and significant platform and station buildings, styled by the line's originators, the Birmingham, Wolverhampton & Dudley Railway and reminiscent of other stations on the line, such as could be seen at West Bromwich, for example. Unfortunately, with the demise of the line in 1972 the station closed and was demolished. However, the opening of the Jewellery Line in 1995, and the Midland Metro in 1999, saw the rails re-laid and the site put to use once again.

▲ Looking towards Birmingham, with the booking office to the right, this undated photograph gives an impression of the size of the station during its operational years. Beyond the waiting rooms, at the end of the Birmingham platform, can be discerned a signal box at the point where the railway crosses Booth Street. *Frank Jennings*

◀ Today the site is unrecognisable from its GWR heyday, the only facilities being two small shelters for Midland Metro passengers. Frank Jennings would have been standing where the shelter to the right stands now, looking towards the camera. To the left are the two 'heavy rail' lines, and to the left of them a scrapyard now occupies what was part of the station and its goods sidings. *14 July 2004*

▶ The only, and not the most appealing, feature of historical significance that exists at the site can be seen in the centre of this photograph of Booth Street, with the station site above – the bricked-up entrance to a gents toilet, and an open-topped one at that! Sadly, as with most of the remaining railway public toilets, it is long-since decommissioned. For those interested, better examples can be seen on Livery Street at Snow Hill and outside the Jewellery Quarter station. *14 July 2004*

The Hawthorns

Grid reference 402515/209733

A newcomer to the local rail scene, The Hawthorns opened in 1995 on the new Jewellery Line, and from 1999 onwards served as a stop for both light and heavy rail with the Midland Metro's Birmingham to Wolverhampton line also passing through the site. From 1931 to 1968 The Hawthorns Halt also stood along this section of track, albeit only Platform 3 catering for return travel to Stourbridge (Platforms 1 and 2 being sited on the other side of Halfords Lane bridge), and accommodated many football specials to the nearby West Bromwich Albion Hawthorns Stadium.

▼ With the possible exception of Bordesley, this is the most uninviting station entrance I have come across in my exploration of the Birmingham railway scene. Resembling something of an 'at Her Majesty's pleasure' establishment, this is the view that greets passengers when arriving at the station from its car park off Carlton Road. *14 July 2004*

▲ Fortunately, things do improve at track level. The overall appearance of the station is of a scaled-down Smethwick Galton Bridge, seen here with the Jewellery Line to the right and, on the other side of the fence, the Midland Metro platforms to the left. *14 July 2004*

▼ This view shows the Midland Metro stop, looking towards Birmingham through the Halfords Lane road bridge – Platforms 1 and 2 of The Hawthorns Halt once stood at this spot. A Class 158 DMU pulls away from the station en route to Stourbridge Junction. *14 July 2004*

West Bromwich

Grid reference 400422/290952

The station opened in 1854 with the GWR's Snow Hill to Wolverhampton Low Level line, promoted by the Birmingham, Wolverhampton & Dudley Railway, and was of significant size with a goods yard, relief lines and an imposing station building and signal box. The station closed with the line in 1972 and all buildings were demolished within months. The platforms, however, lived on, as the trackbed, once the track had been lifted, served as a 'walkway' and remained thus until the late 1990s when clearance work began in preparation for the Midland Metro, which was to open in 1999. Unfortunately – but understandably when the height of the Metro tramcars are considered – the old platforms were finally removed some 27 years after they had last seen rail usage.

▲ This view of West Bromwich taken during the late 1960s shows the station, complete with porter's trolley, looking towards Birmingham as the rails head off under Lyng Lane bridge. The goods facilities here lay hidden behind the wall to the left, and the station building, of BW&DR design, is a facsimile of the one that once stood at Handsworth & Smethwick station. *Frank Jennings*

▶ In this modern view from Lyng Lane bridge, the station building stood to the left, and the wall marking the boundary between passenger and goods facilities is still standing. The goods sidings fanned out to the right, and after they were lifted the site was turned into a warehouse and car park. The Midland Metro stop ahead seems dwarfed by its surroundings! *21 January 2004*

▲ The entrance to the Metro stop on West Bromwich Ringway features a self-explanatory memento of the site's previous incarnation. *21 January 2004*

Route 10: Snow Hill to Olton

Snow Hill – see Route 9, pages 96-100

Moor Street

Grid reference 407425/286790

Like Snow Hill, Moor Street station is a rare example of a railway phoenix from the ashes. Originally opened in 1909 by the GWR, the station was built as the terminus for the new North Warwickshire line and to relieve pressure on Snow Hill, to which it was connected via a

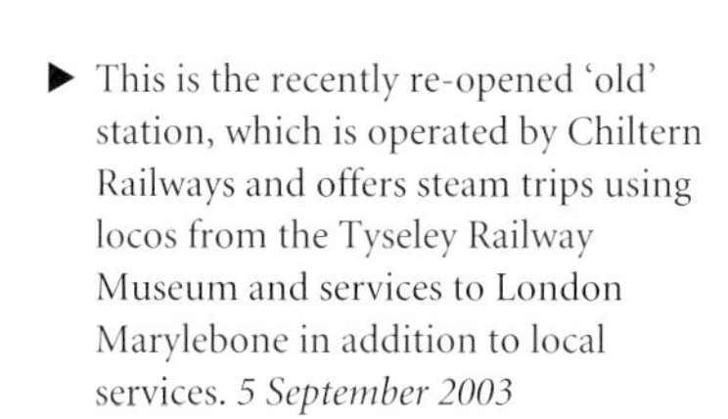

▶ This is the recently re-opened 'old' station, which is operated by Chiltern Railways and offers steam trips using locos from the Tyseley Railway Museum and services to London Marylebone in addition to local services. *5 September 2003*

tunnel. The station was given significant goods facilities and made use of a rare piece of railway engineering – a traverser to move locos from one line to another in the bay platform.

When the tunnel link between Snow Hill and Moor Street closed in 1968, and the goods depot was demolished, Moor Street rapidly became a dilapidated and overgrown 'forgotten' station in the centre of Birmingham. Eventual closure of the old station came in 1987, with the opening that year of a new facility comprising two platforms on the lines that led directly to the tunnel to Snow Hill, and a new entrance.

▶ During the station's twilight years ex-GWR No 6000 *King George V* stands at Moor Street – under police protection. The goods shed, to the left, was then still extant, but disused. The train is standing on a terminus line, as is the policeman, with the lines to the right being the original through lines to Snow Hill. *March 1972; Roger Shenton*

▲ The interior of the booking hall has been very sympathetically renovated and retains a strong GWR feel, as can be seen in this photograph taken shortly after re-opening. For anyone who remembers the state of the station during the late 1970s and early 1980s, Chiltern Railways have done a remarkably good job! *5 September 2003*

▶ Looking in the opposite direction during the station's renovation it is noticeable that the good shed is no more, and there is a car park in its place (as is nearly always the case when goods facilities are removed). In the background is ex-GWR '28xx' Class 2-8-0 8F heavy freight loco No 2885 on loan from Tyseley Railway Museum; at the end of Platform 3, to the left, a water tower has been installed for the steam excursions planned for the station. *5 September 2003*

6000

Bordesley

Grid reference 408445/286030

Bordesley station opened in 1855 with the opening of the GWR's Birmingham to Oxford line (Small Heath and Tyseley did not open until some time later). At first glance it is one of the most uninviting stations I have visited. Built entirely on a viaduct, it was a significant structure comprising a cattle station and goods yard, as well as the passenger station itself. Unfortunately, the station has been considerably run down, with only one island platform remaining in use and the significant canopied platform buildings removed; there is now an extremely sparse timetable for stopping trains and the station has been relegated to an unstaffed halt.

◀ ▼ Seen here are the less-than-inviting entrance to the station from Coventry Road, and a platform view illustrating the total desolation and abandonment of the station, looking towards Small Heath. The Camp Hill line crosses in the distance and there is a former goods warehouse beyond. The island platform on the left is long out of use and crumbling, with all its original buildings removed. The 'concrete bunker'-style waiting room on the operational platform is the only structure at the station; to the extreme right is the entrance to the stairwell leading down to Coventry Road. *24 March 2004*

▲ A short walk around the perimeter of the site reveals much still of interest at the former GWR station. On the corner of Coventry Road and Upper Trinity Street the painted sign seen here still points to the long-closed cattle station, the entrance to which can still be negotiated. The cattle station itself occupied land in the mouth of the never-completed Duddeston Viaduct, built in 1846, which ends abruptly a short walk away. *24 March 2004*

▼ Walking further along Upper Trinity Street to its junction with Adderley Street reveals another relic painted on the side of the Duddeston Viaduct: 'Bordesley Cattle Station – GWR'. Through the bridge can also be seen the viaduct carrying the GWR line from Bordesley, which is to the left, into Moor Street. These interesting finds, and the sheer scale of the viaducts constructed to support the line and station, still make the site worthy of a visit! *24 March 2004*

Small Heath

Grid reference 409703/285058

Small Heath station was opened by the GWR in 1863 as 'Small Heath & Sparkbrook', and from its early days took on a role of a goods station that also dealt with passenger traffic, such was the extent of goods facilities at the site. Today, certainly on the side of the Golden Hillock Road bridge occupied by the platforms themselves, you would be hard pressed to see obvious signs of its industrial past.

◀ The entrance building on Golden Hillock Road gives access to a single island platform serving local services to and from the city centre. It is easy to see that some alterations to the building frontage have taken place over the years – the large white areas on the front topped with concrete lintels were clearly doorways or windows at some time. The left-hand set correspond with the now-locked stairwell down to the original platform for local trains travelling to the Oxford & Birmingham line or the North Warwickshire line, while more illustrious locos such as 'Kings' passed by heading Paddington to Birkenhead expresses. *7 January 2004*

▼ Looking down from Golden Hillock Rd, on the left, adjoining the now disused platform, is the up main line that carried the Leamington and London services. To the left is the line that once formed the exit from the up yard, which joined the main line at Small Heath South signal box just beyond the platform's end – the box no longer exists. The lines on the extreme right were used for goods wagon storage and marshalling in the goods yard proper, on the other side of Golden Hillock Road bridge. *7 January 2004*

▲ This is the site of the goods yards, again seen from Golden Hillock Road, with the station building behind us. In all, the site could accommodate about 2,450 wagons, and was organised into a series of yards for specific purposes: the Caledonian Yard for LNWR/LMS traffic, holding 480 wagons; a transhipment yard holding 360 wagons; and the North End Mileage Yard, holding 70 wagons for the on-site metals shed, among others. Interestingly, Small Heath was even a technologically advanced station – although one could never tell to look at it now. In 1957 a Universal Chain Conveyor was installed, which kept three chains permanently circulating along channels in the main shed at a speed of 40 feet per minute to haul wagons around on their cycle from loaded to empty without unnecessary handling/shunting being required. *7 January 2004*

Tyseley

Grid reference 411010/284035

Originally opened in 1906 by the GWR, Tyseley station stood on what was then the Snow Hill to Leamington and Paddington line. However, with the opening of the North Warwickshire line in 1908, Tyseley's traffic considerably increased. In addition to this, and possibly reflecting its new-found importance, significant goods facilities and the 'legendary' Tyseley loco shed and associated loco works were built here too.

▶ The booking office is perched above the track on Wharfedale Road and, as is apparent from this photograph, has been well preserved due, in part, to the station now serving as the hub for the nearby Tyseley Railway Museum and a modicum of railway works still occupying part of the site. *7 January 2004*

▲ Looking down from Wharfedale Road, with the booking office off-camera to the left, the disused perimeter of the site can be discerned. The overgrown and disused sidings extend deep into the area ahead and to the left, which now houses some small industrial units and a lorry park. This area formed the goods side of the station site, with the other side, to the extreme left, accommodating the railway works and shed. *7 January 2004*

▼ Standing on Platform 3, looking towards Birmingham, we can see that Platforms 1 and 2 on the right are, although immaculately maintained, disused. The extent of the preservation of the site is apparent: note the darted valances to the canopies and the total absence of graffiti and litter! A short wander around the station reveals many artefacts of the station's heritage, such as wrought-iron GWR benches. *7 January 2004*

Acocks Green

Grid reference 412400/283490

Acocks Green opened in 1852 on the GWR's Oxford & Birmingham Branch, and was renamed 'Acocks Green & South Yardley in 1878 only to return to plain Acocks Green some years later. Unlike Tyseley, this station has been stripped of not only much of its character but also its tracks.

▲ The booking office remains fairly intact, apart from the bricking-up of its entrances to the right and left (behind the van), so my hopes of finding a well-maintained period station were raised – but were soon dashed. At track level this previously large suburban station is a shadow of its former self, now consisting of a single island platform serving the route between Leamington Spa and Great Malvern. *7 January 2004*

▶ This is the view looking towards Leamington Spa, with the booking office to the right. It is not immediately apparent what has been lost at the station over the years; however, to the right stood another island platform and sidings, the land now having been reclaimed for the car park, and at the furthest end of the site a footbridge spanned the tracks. *7 January 2004*

▲ A look of the rear of the booking office gives some idea of what has been removed, with the stairwell to the left now leading to the car park. Two relief lines used the disused and fenced-off archway in the bridge ahead, installed in the inter-war years to handle the increased freight traffic and the expanding commuter demands from the city's suburbs. To get an impression of the site in its heyday, the platform facilities here rivalled those that can still be seen at Tyseley today. *7 January 2004*

Olton

Grid reference 413382/282312

Despite some considerable 'rationalisation' of track and buildings over the years, this ex-GWR station, opened in 1869, has retained some character and points of historical interest, not least its booking office.

▲ The booking office on Station Drive is an original feature of the station, with entry to the platforms being gained from a tunnel that, surprisingly for station facilities in the region, is remarkably clean, and even decorated with hanging baskets! *7 January 2004*

► At track level, which lies on a low embankment, a sorry scene greets visitors. The station has been reduced to a single island platform, with one original building, obscured by the top of the lift-shaft nearest the camera in this view, and a second platform now out of use. *7 January 2004*

Route 11: Snow Hill to Shirley

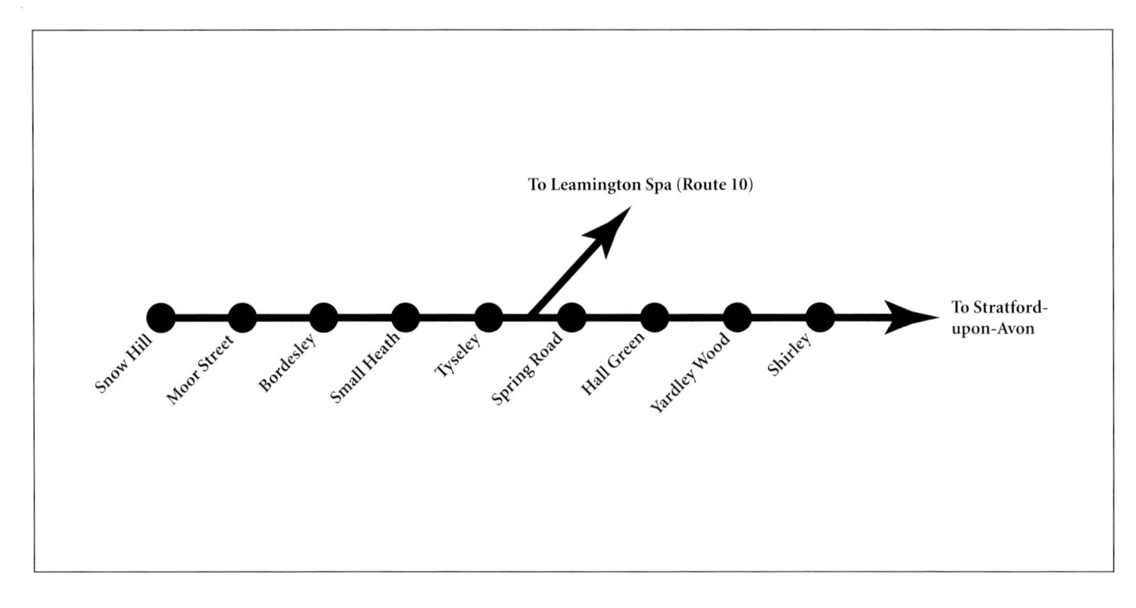

Snow Hill – see Route 9, pages 96-100

Moor Street, Bordesley, Small Heath, Tyseley – see Route 10, pages 111-118

Spring Road

Grid reference 411205/282935

One of the stranger stations in the region, for reasons that will become apparent, is the former GWR 'Spring Road Platform', opened in 1908 on the North Warwickshire line as the first stop after the junction with the main line at Tyseley. The current station has been slightly truncated from GWR days due to the construction of a multi-storey car park over the tracks.

◀ The somewhat odd-looking 'garden shed' structure used to be the ticket office, but is now disused and a 'Portakabin' has been erected for this purpose just the other side of it and out of shot. Quite how this somewhat unique structure has survived the years is unknown, but it is the sole period structure at the station today. *7 January 2004*

▶ This view, taken from Spring Road bridge looking towards Stratford, shows the aforementioned multi-storey car park looming in the distance. The car park spanning the tracks is not of railway build or usage, but privately owned by a factory that encompasses part of the surrounding area, and its construction necessitated some remodelling of the station from its GWR days. *7 January 2004*

Hall Green

Grid reference 410590/282110

Good examples of GWR stations in the Birmingham area are few and far between today, but Hall Green, opened in 1908 on the then new North Warwickshire line, is an exception. Sitting in what was, and to an extent still is, a leafy suburb of Birmingham, the station was on a grand scale and, apart from losing its goods yard, remains largely intact.

▼ Apart from some signs of neglect and the loss of what were at best meagre facilities on the Stratford platform, nothing much has changed inside the station over the last 100 years. Here we see the station building and entrance from the car park in Station Drive – compare this building with those at Henley-in-Arden and Shirley to get a good perspective of GWR architecture at the turn of the last century. *7 January 2004*

▲ Viewed from the footbridge looking towards Birmingham, the area of land immediately beyond the platform to the left accommodated the goods yard and a coal merchant. The goods facilities here also operated a Passenger's Luggage in Advance service, which offered a home pick-up for items passengers wished to be sent ahead to their destination. *7 January 2004*

▼ The station building is remarkably well-preserved, albeit under-used in terms of its facilities, now only operating for the purchasing of tickets. The darted valance along the canopy edge is a feature from the GWR period that unfortunately has been long-since removed from many stations. *7 January 2004*

Yardley Wood

Grid reference 409980/280345

The station was opened by the GWR with the line in 1908 as 'Yardley Wood Platform' – 'platform' being a term peculiar to the GWR to describe a hybrid of 'halt' and 'station'. The surrounding area had been awaiting a station since 1894, when the ill-fated Birmingham, North Warwickshire & Stratford-upon-Avon Railway first mooted the idea; however, apart from getting the required powers from Parliament to go ahead with the plan, that company foundered on financial grounds (among other things), and the line never materialised. The GWR took up the scheme and reworked the plans, obtaining Parliamentary powers in 1901.

▶ This is the station building on Highfield Road, with the entrance to the Birmingham platform on the left. As evidence of the extent to which the station and the line have largely escaped modernisation over the years, note the railings, gatepost and chimney stacks! *7 January 2004*

▼ Looking towards Stratford, one could almost imagine that this is a photograph from the opening of the station, such is the lack of present-day reference points. The waiting rooms and now-disused office and toilets on the Birmingham platform to the right are original features. *7 January 2004*

Shirley

Grid reference 410625/278445

By far the best example of a GWR station still in existence in the Birmingham area is to be found here. The station opened with the North Warwickshire line in 1908 and is a virtual 'time capsule' from that period, having survived the past 100 years relatively unscathed, apart from the inevitable loss of the goods yard.

▶ The view towards Stratford shows the footbridge and, beyond it, the Haslucks Green Road overbridge. Apart from the station signs, nothing appears out of place from when the GWR was running the station – even down to the use of semaphore signals! There is a real feeling here that an effort has been made to preserve the station's appearance, even extending to the placing and upkeep of plant tubs on the platforms. *7 January 2004*

▲ Here we see the station building from the car park off Green Road, which is typical of the other large stations on the line (see Hall Green, for example). Immediately to the rear of the photographer is the station master's house. *7 January 2004*

▶ Looking back towards Birmingham we can see the signal box, which, apart from having UPVC double-glazing, looks remarkably in period and is in fully functioning order – if you stand by it you can hear the wires at track level when the signals are operated! A small siding still exists here off-camera to the left, and the land behind the box, which is now a timber yard, used to be the goods yard over which the signal box also had control. *7 January 2004*

Gentlemen
Ladies
Waiting room
Way out

Shirley

Index of locations